CW01630695

a taste of

Maltese Folklore

tradition and heritage

a taste of

Maltese Folklore

tradition and heritage

Joseph C. Camilleri

BDL Publishing

(+356) 2138 0351

www.bdlbooks.com

First edition, 2015
Reprinted, 2018

Editor: Oliver Gatt
Proofreading: Katryna Storace

The author wishes to thank Mr Anton Miceli, an official personnel from the Ministry of Culture, for his help regarding the Malta Summer Carnival; Mr Martin Azzopardi (*Is-Serkin*) who owns Crystal Palace *pastizzi* shop in Rabat; Mr George Sammut. A special word of thanks goes to the author's wife, Grace Camilleri.

A Taste of **Maltese Folklore,**
Tradition and Heritage

pg 17 – Mark Vella
pg 84 – Patrick J. Fenech
pgs 114–119 – Michael Cassar
pg 132 – www.thisishush.com
pgs 142, 148 – Mark Micallef

Previous page: A nonagenarian cloistered nun in St Catherine's monastery, Valletta.

ISBN: 978-99957-46-60-5

Printed by Gutenberg Press, Ħal Tarxien

Contents

Introduction

The Maltese archipelago consists of a number of small islands – mainly Malta (the main island), Gozo, Comino, Cominotto, St Paul's Islands, Filfla and Manoel Island. Only Malta, Gozo and Comino are inhabited. This archipelago lies in the middle of the Mediterranean Sea. These islands are almost arid, rocky and devoid of natural resources, except for globigerina limestone, which is used for building and sea salt. However, since this archipelago is blessed with many hours of sunshine, solar energy has been developed in recent years.

Parched fields lined with rubble walls and agrobuildings, such as the *girna* and the *razzett*, are distinctive and form an integral part of the Maltese countryside. Typical villages, with their flat-roofed houses and small chapels in narrow streets and alleys have survived. These still have their characteristic tiny shop full of items for sale jammed right up to its entrance. The village greengrocer and the baker still exist along these streets. In these villages, the most dominant feature is the baroque parish church with its bell towers and the dome reaching towards the blue sky. The heart of these villages is the main square enclosed by townhouses, buildings housing band and political parties clubs, and traditional bars serving *pastizzi* and coffee or tea. Even the parish priest's office is usually found in or near this square, while the local police station is often located in a nearby street. Every old village has its own 'Main Street',

An old Maltese gentleman enjoys a quiet moment in Valletta.

which in the past was referred to by the locals as '*Stradarjali*' ('Kingsway'). In this street one sees more townhouses and possibly other old chapels and a shop or two.

Large old towns also continue to breathe. Some of them were elevated to the status of city either by the Grandmasters of the Order of St John of Jerusalem, Rhodes and Malta, or by the British. A few of these cities were surrounded by kilometres of defence walls, making them gems of fortified cities. Cases in point are Mdina, Valletta and its suburb Floriana, the Three Cities (Vittoriosa, Cospicua and Senglea) and Gozo's Citadella.

The Maltese archipelago supports a large population that has created its own characteristics, distinguishing itself from its neighbours in Sicily and North Africa. These characteristics are the centre of attraction for the visiting tourist who is keen to get to know Malta better during his or her stay. Some have been included in this book to help the reader to better appreciate the Maltese heritage – a heritage which was handed down from one generation to another, making the Maltese archipelago unique and at the same time European and Mediterranean.

The traditional Maltese tile is still being crafted by hand.

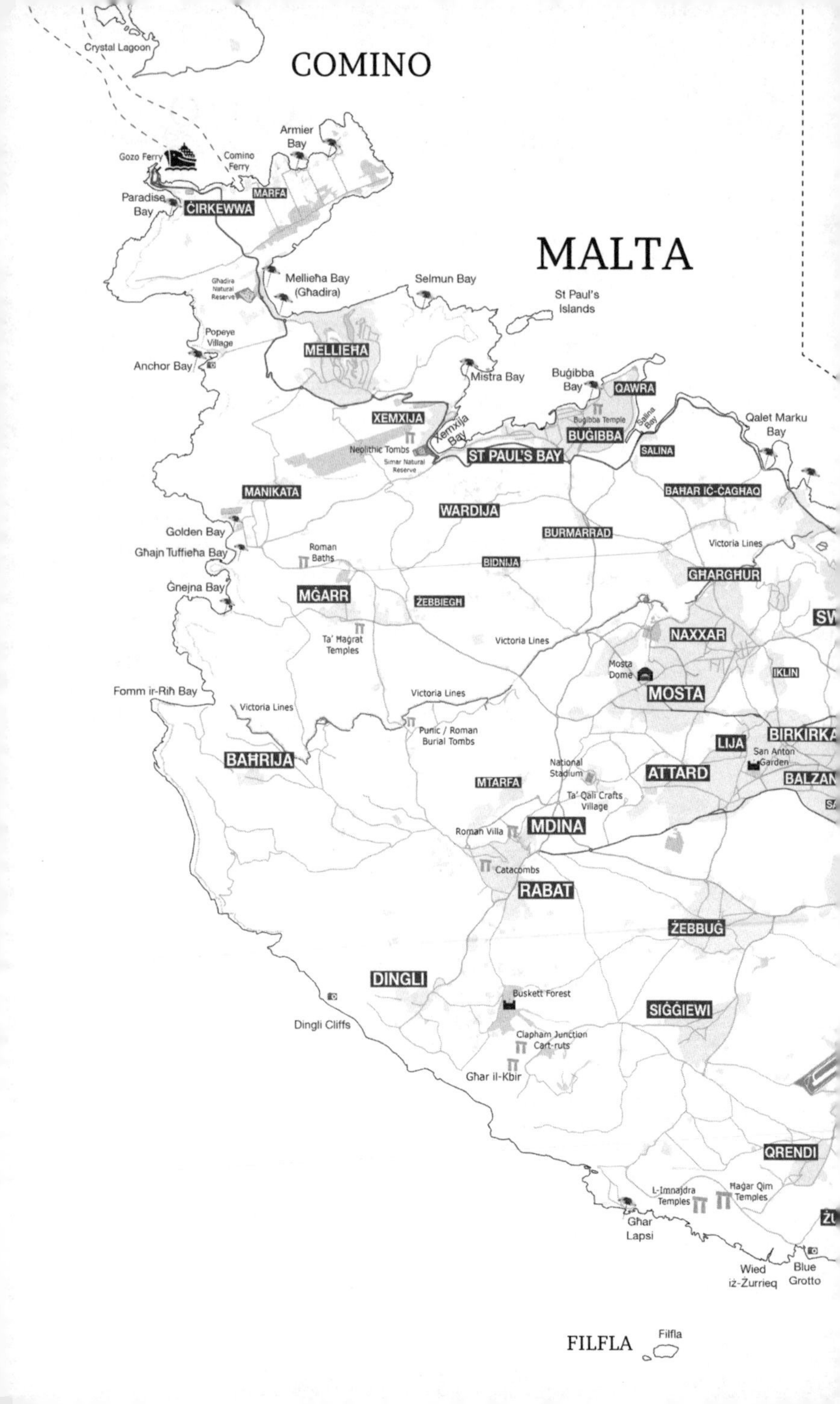

COMINO
Crystal Lagoon
MALTA
Armier Bay
Gozo Ferry
Comino Ferry
MARFA
Paradise Bay
ĊIRKEWWA
Mellieħa Bay (Għadira)
Selmun Bay
Għadira Natural Reserve
St Paul's Islands
Popeye Village
MELLIEĦA
Anchor Bay
Mistra Bay
Buġibba Bay
QAWRA
XEMXIJA
Buġibba Temple
Salina Bay
Qalet Marku Bay
Xemxija Bay
BUĠIBBA
Neolithic Tombs
Simar Natural Reserve
ST PAUL'S BAY
SALINA
MANIKATA
BAĦAR IĊ-ĊAGĦAQ
WARDIJA
Golden Bay
BURMARRAD
Għajn Tuffieħa Bay
Roman Baths
Victoria Lines
BIDNIJA
GĦARGĦUR
Ġnejna Bay
MĠARR
ŻEBBIEGĦ
Ta' Ħaġrat Temples
Victoria Lines
NAXXAR
Mosta Dome
IKLIN
Fomm ir-Riħ Bay
Victoria Lines
MOSTA
Victoria Lines
Punic / Roman Burial Tombs
LIJA
BAĦRIJA
San Anton Garden
National Stadium
ATTARD
MTARFA
Ta' Qali Crafts Village
Roman Villa
MDINA
Catacombs
RABAT
ŻEBBUĠ
DINGLI
Buskett Forest
SIĠĠIEWI
Dingli Cliffs
Clapham Junction Cart-ruts
Għar il-Kbir
QRENDI
L-Imnajdra Temples
Ħaġar Qim Temples
Għar Lapsi
Wied iż-Żurrieq
Blue Grotto
FILFLA
Filfla

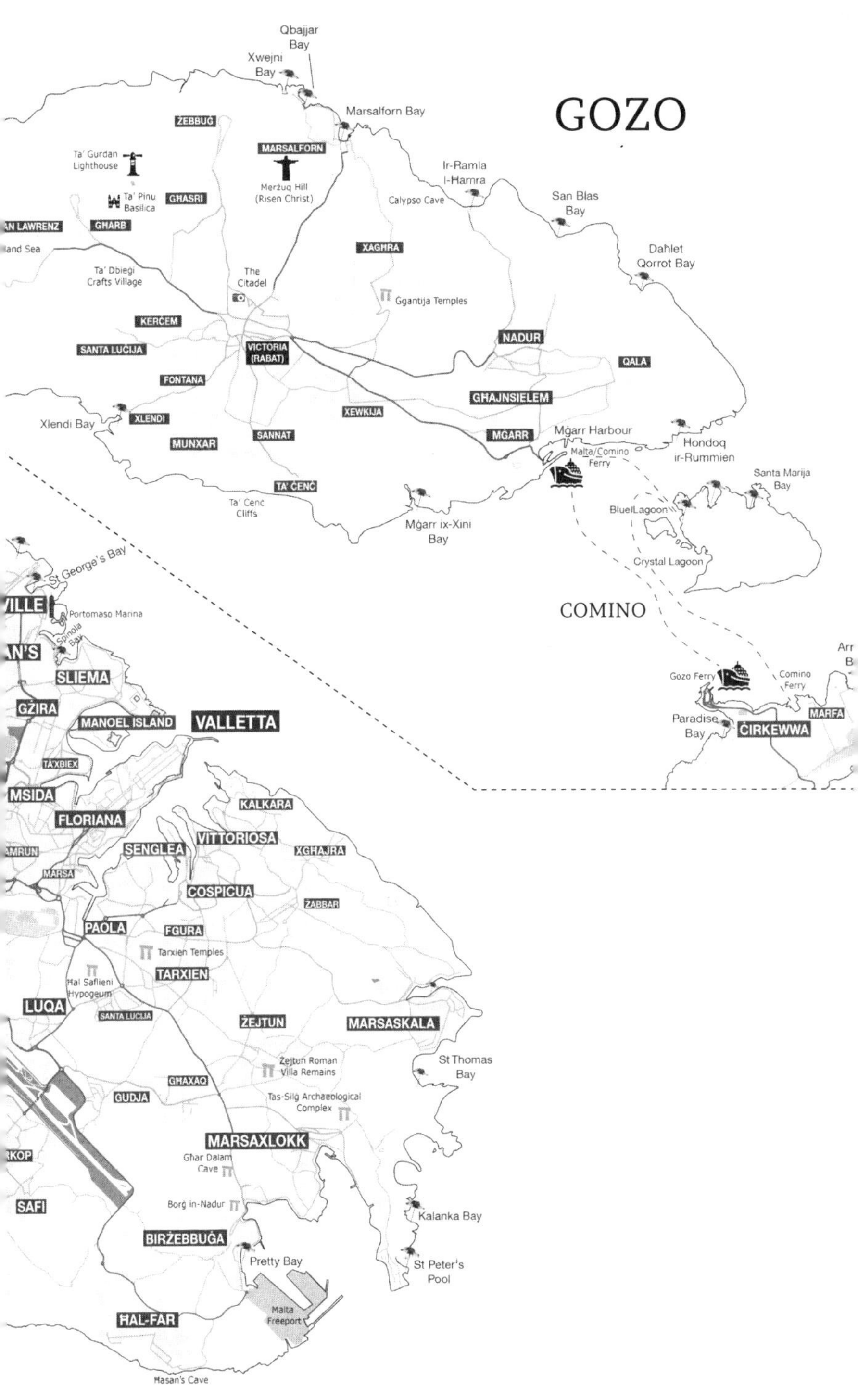

GOZO
Qbajjar Bay
Xwejni Bay
Marsalforn Bay
ŻEBBUĠ
MARSALFORN
Ta' Gurdan Lighthouse
Merżuq Hill (Risen Christ)
Ir-Ramla l-Ħamra
Ta' Pinu Basilica
GĦASRI
Calypso Cave
San Blas Bay
GĦARB
XAGĦRA
Dahlet Qorrot Bay
Ta' Dbiegi Crafts Village
The Citadel
Ġgantija Temples
KERĊEM
NADUR
SANTA LUĊIJA
VICTORIA (RABAT)
QALA
FONTANA
GĦAJNSIELEM
Xlendi Bay
XLENDI
XEWKIJA
MĠARR
Mġarr Harbour
SANNAT
Hondoq ir-Rummien
MUNXAR
Malta/Comino Ferry
TA' ĊENĊ
Santa Marija Bay
Ta' Ċenċ Cliffs
Blue Lagoon
Mġarr ix-Xini Bay
Crystal Lagoon
COMINO
St George's Bay
Portomaso Marina
Spinola Bay
Gozo Ferry
Comino Ferry
SLIEMA
MARFA
GŻIRA
Paradise Bay
ĊIRKEWWA
MANOEL ISLAND
VALLETTA
TA'XBIEX
MSIDA
KALKARA
FLORIANA
VITTORIOSA
SENGLEA
XGĦAJRA
MARSA
COSPICUA
ŻABBAR
PAOLA
FGURA
Tarxien Temples
TARXIEN
Ħal Saflieni Hypogeum
LUQA
SANTA LUĊIJA
ŻEJTUN
MARSASKALA
Żejtun Roman Villa Remains
St Thomas Bay
GĦAXAQ
GUDJA
Tas-Silġ Archaeological Complex
MARSAXLOKK
Għar Dalam Cave
SAFI
Borġ in-Nadur
Kalanka Bay
BIRŻEBBUĠA
Pretty Bay
St Peter's Pool
Malta Freeport
ĦAL-FAR
Ħasan's Cave

The Maltese Islands

The National Colours

The Constitution lays down that the National Flag '…consists of two equal vertical stripes, white in the hoist and red in the fly.' It also includes a representation of the George Cross, which was awarded to the Maltese, by the British monarch, King George VI, during the horrible days of the Second World War. This cross is edged in red and placed in the canton of the white stripe.

Not all scholars agree on the origin of these colours. Some are of the opinion that these were given to the Maltese by Count Roger of Hauteville when he landed in Malta in 1090 to liberate the Islands from Arab control – the white-and-red being part of his family's coat of arms. Others argue that these colours were given to the Maltese by the Aragonese monarch, King Alfonso V, in 1428.

One of the Norman legends expresses popular belief that the colours were passed on to us by Count Roger who, as Joseph Cassar Pullicino writes in his *Norman Legends in Malta* and published in the magazine, *Scientia* (1945): 'It is a widespread and deeply implanted belief in Malta that the white and red colours of the National Flag were bestowed by Count Roger

A house in an alley, Mdina.

The Maltese flag flutters atop the Auberge de Castile, Valletta.

who, having freed the island from the Arabs, raised Malta to the rank of a small nation, granting it the privilege of its own banner and shield.' This legend states that the colours are supposed to have originated from the Count's coat of arms, when in fact, in 1090, armorial bearings were still unknown. Moreover, Goffredo Malaterra, the Count's scribe, did not refer to them at all.

The King Alfonso story is supported by a document kept in the Mdina Cathedral Archives. This document states that in 1428, on the occasion of a visit of ambassadors from Malta to Valencia, the Maltese representatives asked the sovereign for an official shield. E. R. Leopardi notes, in his publication, *Malta's Heritage* (1969), that: 'The king pointed to his chest clothed in white, then holding forward his red cape he said; "these colours will be your shield and your flag."' Unfortunately, this document dating from the 18th century does not include any references to the original manuscript.

In Mdina, Malta's ancient capital, we find traces of these colours. The baptismal font at the Cathedral contains the white-and-red shield. This font belongs to the Norman Cathedral destroyed by an earthquake in 1693. The former Norman Cathedral's main wooden door, which is well preserved as a sacristy door at present, includes the white-and-red shield carved into it. This door is dates back to 1520. Finally, the Cathedral Museum, which is located a few metres away from the Cathedral, houses pieces of art that include the white-and-red shield.

The George Cross, on display at the Military History Museum, Fort St Elmo.

Moreover, in the Mdina Cathedral Annunciation chapel, there is a large painting commemorating the deliverance of Malta from a siege with North African corsairs. In this painting we see St Paul flying on a white horse, fighting the corsairs. As a background, there is a walled city flying a white-and-red flag.

The Rubble Walls (*Il-Ħitan tas-Sejjieħ*)

One of the characteristics of the Maltese countryside is the rubble wall (also known as 'rock wall'). These walls divide fields into small portions in which the farmer grows vegetables and fruit for the local markets, as well as onions and potatoes for export. Grapes, Malta's cash crop, are also grown.

In some areas rubble walls are low – less than two metres high – while in other areas they could be much higher. These walls serve various functions. They mark the contours of fields, pathways, terrain and open spaces. They also preserve the soil acting as a sieve, allowing rainwater to flow through while holding back the soil. Moreover, rubble walls provide a home for many species of flora and fauna. The caper plant is a case in point. This plant's buds are very popular in the Maltese kitchen as they provide a distant flavour to many local dishes.

A rubble wall located in the limits of Marsaskala.

These walls also provide living quarters for bees, butterflies and lizards. Tall rubble walls also serve as windbreakers for fruit trees.

Some scholars believe that these walls originated in prehistoric times. Paul Portelli claims in his article 'Rubble Walls' published in the magazine *Malta This Month* in July 2000: 'They were probably first built on hilltops to keep soil, which was carted up from the valleys by the first farmers, from eroding.' The stones used for erecting these walls are collected from nearby fields. It is important to note that these walls do not include any mortar.

We find two types of walls – the single leaf and the double leaf walls. The material used in the construction of these walls varies as it depends on the geographic and geologic elements found in the area. In the north of Malta, the most common material used is the *Ġebla tax-Xagħri* or *Gagazza*. Some rubble wall builders consider this stone as the best stone for the job. In the south, the globigerina limestone (*tal-franka*) is used. Usually, the material for rubble walls in this part of Malta is made up of discarded quarry material know as *Xripp* or *Inforra*. This material consists of the upper layer of a quarry, which is not suitable for building purposes. Moreover, in the south, rubble walls are finished with 'franka chippings' ('*Laqx*'), which are used as wedges (*feles*) to fill in gap and fissures.

In order to erect these walls one has to have specific tools. These consist mainly of a spade and a sort of hatchet (*Imterqa tal-Inkulmar*), which is in fact a double-edged walling hammer. Its edges are used for rough shaping and stone dressing.

To erect a rubble wall one must first lay the foundation stones. The wall's direction is guided by a string (*ħjut* or *lenza*) tied to pieces of wooden poles. The foundation stones are large and placed in such a way that narrow gaps are left to serve as water filters. Next, smaller stones are used to form layers over the large stones. The worker has a set of rules to follow. The head (*ras*) side of the stone has to be placed facing the external part of the wall, while the tail (*denb*) faces the inside of the wall. In the case of double leaf walls, a gap is created and filled with *mazkan*, which consists of stone and rock fragments. These serve for binding. To strengthen the wall, bond stones (*ktajjen*) are placed at intervals of about two metres, linking the two leafs for greater stability. This is further strengthened by the small pieces of wood (*ħatab*). This wood has a dual function: first, to absorb water and also, to prevent pressure on the wall's surface.

During the British Rule, two types of stones were added to the rubble walls. One of these was the milestone built by the British Military to help soldiers find their location. The second type was boundary stone, which marked the lands belonging to the Royal British Crown. Most of these carried the monogram of King George VI.

In view of their historical and architectural importance, rubble walls and their surroundings are considered to be part of the Maltese heritage and they are part and parcel of the Maltese conservation areas.

The Corbelled Stone Hut (*Il-Girna*)

All over Malta rubble walls surround fields. In the western and northwestern parts of the island, these walls are further enriched by corbelled stone huts (*girna* in the singular, or *giren* in the plural). This corbelled stone hut consists of a single room with double walls of undressed stones which are unplastered. Its ceiling is in the shape of a dome. The roof is covered with fragments of rock and stone, and at times also with sand and lime. Ground pottery (*deffun*) is rarely used.

There are different shapes of *girna*: the circular type as well as the square or rectangular type. Oval shaped *giren* are rarely

A *girna* in the northern part of Malta.

found. Some of the largest circular *giren* are located along the fields and rocky ground between the Red Tower at Northern Mellieħa and Ċirkewwa. On the other hand, the largest square *giren* are found at ix-Xagħra l-Ħamra in the limits of Manikata, another area of Mellieħa.

As most of the *giren* are located in the west and north-west of Malta, the stone used in their construction is coralline limestone, which is available on the surface together with soil. The most important part of the *girna* is the slab over the door. This can be horizontal, arched or triangular in shape.

There is no rule regarding the size, height or width of the *girna*. These all depend on the needs of the farmer or herdsman who commissioned its construction. It also depended on the skills of the corbelled stone hut builder.

According to Fr Michael Fsadni, in his article 'The Girna, corbelled stone hut', published in the magazine *Malta This Month* of November 1993, some corbelled stone huts were also

Interior view of a *girna* showing the dome-shaped ceiling and doorway.

used for residential purposes. This seems rather impossible, as these constructions are too small to accommodate all the members of the family. On the other hand, the *girna* catered for all the personal needs of the farmer or herdsman. Sometimes, the farmer had to work land which was not within walking distance of his farmhouse, so the farmer had to find a place to store agricultural tools as well as the food and drink he took with him. In the *girna,* the farmer also kept some of the crops he wished to sell on the local market. Potatoes, onions, hay and other products were often stored there. Moreover, the roof of the *girna* was sometimes used to dry figs, tomatoes and carobs in the sun.

The herdsman would use also the *girna* during grazing time for keeping his food and drink. Both the farmer and the herdsman took refuge from the strong rays of the summer sun or sudden downpours, which are very common during the autumn season.

The *giren* are no longer used by farmers or herdsmen: some were lost by weathering, but a number still survive. Both the *giren* and the dry stone walls (*ħitan tas-sejjieħ*) are part of the conservation areas of the Maltese countryside.

Niches

Malta's towns, villages, hamlets and the countryside are rich in niches. Sometimes, one meets a niche along some narrow winding street or at the beginning of a sheltered alley. At other times, one can see them among rubble walls along countryside paths. We find two types of niches: those which have a cover and those that are free standing. These niches stand testimony to the faith of the Maltese through the ages.

There are all sorts of niches: some have small or life-size figures of Christ, the Blessed Virgin or the saints; others show

A street corner niche in the old part of Victoria, Gozo.

the Souls of Purgatory. These usually enrich rubble walls which lie within a stone's throw from the locality's cemetery or decorate a cemetery wall itself. Some recent niches feature just a cross and the name of a person with dates marking a fatal accident. Niches became popular in Malta when the new capital city was being built in the 16th century. The Knights of St John, who ruled Malta at that time, ordered that whoever wanted to build a corner dwelling in Valletta had to embellish it either by some wall decoration or by erecting a niche.

Niches have several functions. Firstly, they offer the opportunity for the faithful to express their beliefs in public. The locals decorate these niches with flowers and lit candles. Sometimes, electric bulbs are lit during the evening, which enhance the area around the niche. Another function is that of providing a familiar landmark to the locals. Whenever someone wishes to meet another person, they would often decide on a particular niche as a meeting place, as this would be well known by the locals. Niches also decorate house façades, countryside rubble walls and town or village squares.

There are several reasons why people built niches. There were the members of the upper middle class who liked to inform everybody in the town or village that they had the means to erect these public shrines. There were also members of a lay confraternity who wished to demonstrate to all the villagers and townspeople that their fraternity worked hard to spread the devotion towards their patron saint. Finally, there were those who made a vow for the recovery of a member of the family from a serious illness or for the deliverance from a plague or some other dreadful disease.

Usually, next to the niche, a plaque is fixed stating a number of days' indulgence granted to those who stop for a

A baroque niche in the village of Ħal Għaxaq with the Archangel Michael trampling Satan.

while to offer a prayer. Some niches have also become famous. Valletta has two famous niches which decorate the corners of St John's and St Paul's streets depicting St Michael and St Paul respectively. The Attard parish church façade – a gem of a baroque church – has several niches. The figure of St Paul is often featured in niches especially in Rabat, St Paul's Bay and Naxxar. Gudja's main square boasts two large niches featuring Our Lady and St Joseph, while Tarxien has a special large niche in the outskirts of the village dedicated to the Annunciation of Our Lady, the patron saint of the village. Finally, one must not forget to mention a special niche found on the islands of St Paul, built to commemorate the apostle's shipwreck in the nearby bay.

Niches created a new demand in the field of the arts: Maltese artists were being asked to create a figure of a saint to decorate a façade or a square. Many Maltese sculptors were involved in this art, which entailed the sculpturing of a globigerina limestone block of stone. Names like Mariano Gerada, Alexandro Farrugia and Wistin Camilleri, to mention a few, are all connected with commissions to create some limestone figures of a particular saint. A case in point is Mariano Gerada who, after sculpturing the titular statues of the Żabbar and Żurrieq parishes, was later asked to sculpt two other similar figures to decorate a main street in Żabbar and the parish church side square in Żurrieq.

Niches are part of the Maltese patrimony and they should be well preserved for future generations.

Chapels

Many towns and villages, as well as the Maltese countryside, possess a good number of chapels. Their domes and bell towers seem to compete with each other to reach the blue Mediterranean sky. This bit of heritage, it seems, all started from cave churches.

At first, caves were used as living quarters for the family or to shelter animals during the night. By time, the Maltese started to use caves as places of worship. The first cave chapel

St Paul's Grotto, Rabat, where tradition holds that the saint passed his time after the shipwreck in 60 A.D.

is still functioning. According to tradition, it is believed that the former Roman prison next to the Mdina–Rabat Roman wall was the first church in Malta. In this cave, the apostle Paul spent his three-month sojourn in Malta. This cave – also known as St Paul's Grotto – is located underneath the Rabat parish church dedicated to the saint.

Another grotto chapel is found underneath the Dominican church of Our Lady of the Cave, also at Rabat. This cave chapel is reached by a flight of steps from the main church. Inside the chapel there is a marble figure of Our Lady and baby Jesus. One of the local legends states that a hunter took refuge in this cave during a hunting session. He fell asleep and slept there for many days – some say even a couple of years. In his sleep, he dreamt that he saw the image of our Lady. When he awoke he realised that he had been inside the cave all that time. After relating his story, the devotion towards Our Lady at that

St Basil and St Michael chapels in Mqabba.

Our Lady of Providence chapel, Siġġiewi.

location of the cave started to grow. Later, this developed into the present devotion towards Our Lady of the Cave.

Mellieħa has another famous cave chapel. In this chapel, one finds a Marian fresco on one of the cave's walls depicting Our Lady and baby Jesus underneath which an altar was erected. Part of the cave ceiling is also covered by paintings, while the chapel also has several other altars. Next to this cave chapel there is a museum housing votive offerings the local people commissioned or donated to express their gratitude towards our Lady for a miracle at sea or at work.

There are many other cave chapels throughout Malta, such as the St Paul the Hermit chapel at Wied il-Għasel, a valley in Mosta.

Some chapels were built either by the locals, by members of the Maltese aristocracy, or by members of the Order of St John. Usually, these chapels were erected to fulfil a vow. The chapel

The church of Our Lady of Mercy, Qrendi.

of Our Lady of Hope at Mosta was built along its valley, Wied l-Isperanza, to fulfil the vow of a young girl who was saved from her fate as a slave at the hands of North Africa corsairs who used to visit our shores to carry off locals to the slave markets of their country. According to a popular legend, the girl managed to escape the sea-pirates and took shelter inside a cave. While hiding she made a vow that if she managed to escape, she would erect a chapel over the cave.

Another popular chapel is found on the outskirts of Gudja along the road adjoining the village of Gudja to Birżebbuġa. A member of the Order of St John made a vow, during a skirmish against sea-pirates, that if he survived, he would build a chapel dedicated to Our Lady of Loreto out of his own pockets. The Maltese and the Knights won the battle and the chapel was built.

There are chapels that were built by some members of the clergy. One such chapel was built at Tarxien, next to the main house of the parish priest. A priest from this locality left a sum of money in his will to erect a chapel dedicated to St Bartolommeo and Our Lady of Good Council. A well-known architect was chosen to prepare the plans. Thanks to his generosity this locality has a gem of a baroque chapel, making Tarxien's main street one of the most important in architectural heritage.

In the countryside, one could come across a chapel standing among the rubble walls and fields. These are the remains of small local communities left uninhabited. By time, farmhouses, *giren* and other countryside buildings came down leaving the chapels as reminders of the village life of centuries gone by. Some of these chapels were main places of worship and they were decorated by medieval frescos depicting saints and

Fresco wall-paintings inside the church of the Annunciation of the Virgin, Ħal Millieri.

biblical scenes. At Ħal Millieri – a deserted hamlet between Żurrieq and Imqabba – there is a chapel dedicated to the Annunciation depicting a series of standing saints. Gudja's former parish church, which was built outside the village core, is also decorated by medieval frescoes.

Some chapels were built to mark a particular devotion towards a saint or hermit connected with the area. Not all of this type of chapels faced the same fate. Some were forgotten by time but others managed to increase the devotion towards the saint and ended up as major religious places of worship. At Qala there is the Immaculate Conception Sanctuary linked with the story of a hermit, San Kurraw (St Corrado). This hermit had to leave Mosta as the local people had turned against him and chased him to the seashore. Legend has it that by a miracle he opened out his cloak and sailed on it to Comino. After living there for some time he grew unhappy and took up residence at Qala.

Another famous chapel, which became a sanctuary is that of Our Lady of Ta' Pinu. A countrywoman, Karmni Grima, used to take her herd to graze in the area of Ta' Pinu, next to Għarb. One day she heard a voice asking her to visit the chapel and pray. This story reached the church authorities and when finally it was officially recognised, a sanctuary was built next to the chapel.

These chapels are part of the Maltese heritage. Some mark an event which occurred many years ago while others are linked to a legend or special devotion.

Stone Crosses

In some localities, we meet a stone column with a cross at the top. Usually, at the base there is a flight of circular steps. These stone crosses either mark special events that occurred throughout the centuries or boundaries between one parish and another. Most of these crosses are associated with traditions that took place annually.

The most famous stone cross is found in Howard Gardens, just outside the Mdina walls. It is located on a spot where the church of St Mark the Evangelist once stood. This church had to be demolished as its location threatened the security of the Mdina walls. Today, the church of St Mark the Evangelist is part of the Augustinian monastery of Rabat. This cross was an important landmark. In medieval times, the magistrate of Mdina used to hold public hearings at this spot. Moreover, it was a customary on Palm Sunday to hold a procession for cathedral chapter members leaving from the Mdina Cathedral and ending at the foot of the cross. For this occasion, the cross used to be decorated with a palm branch and an olive tree branch. After the blessing of these branches, the chapter used to return to the cathedral using the same route.

At Qormi, we find a typical Maltese square in front of Our Lady of the Victories church. In this square, there is another stone cross. It is a reminder of a number of churches that were deconsecrated and demolished on the order of Bishop Balaguer.

Another similar cross was erected at Ħal Millieri in the limits of Żurrieq, next to St John the Evangelist's chapel. In the vicinity of this chapel, there is a second chapel dedicated to the Annunciation. In former days, a third chapel also existed in this area and the stone cross is another reminder of this chapel. At Balzan, there is a street named Three Churches Street. In fact, in this street we only find two churches standing near each

Stone cross located in Safi.

other. One is dedicated to St Rocque and the other is dedicated to the Annunciation. The third church no longer exists and is represented by a stone cross which is located between these two small churches.

The village of Luqa has a stone cross next to the parish church dedicated to the apostle Andrew. This cross commemorates three small churches once demolished so that a new parish church could be erected in the mid-18th century.

Żebbuġ parish church faces a square in which a stone cross was built in a Corinthian style on the plans of Lorenzo Gafà, a famous Maltese architect. This cross marks the creation of a square in front of this monumental church. It was the idea of the then parish priest, Fr Dumink Pace, who dreamt of creating this open space to make it easier for everyone to appreciate the façade of the parish church. It is worthwhile to mention that on the column's shaft there is to be found graffiti which represents some vessels.

Tarxien boasts of another unusual stone cross. It is known as *'Is-Salib tad-Dejma'* (the *Dejma* Cross). According to a legend, this cross was erected to mark the battle between the Turks and Knights and the Maltese forces on the eve of the Great Siege of 1565. The Turks lost the battle and they retired to Marsaxlokk Harbour. When the cross was erected it became a landmark for the *Dejma* soldiers to meet there when they were on duty. This cross was rebuilt several times. The original is located inside the village's cemetery. The present stone cross is located some distance away from the original site. This is highly decorated: the first four Sorrowful Mysteries of the Rosary are sculpted on its plinth. The present cross is the work of Marco Montebello and it was made on the design of Chev. R. Bonnici Calì. Safi and Siġġiewi also have stone crosses which are also known as *'Is-Salib tad-Dejma'* as well.

Kirkop has a stone cross next to the Annunciation chapel. This cross marks the custom when in former days, the burials used to take place in both the parish church as well as the Annunciation chapel. Another stone cross is found at Mqabba, next to the parish church dedicated to the Assumption. This cross was erected to mark the death of Dun Ang Mallia, an Imqabba parish priest who worked hard to build the present parish church. He passed away while he was discussing some construction problems with the mason.

Some stone crosses were built to mark the demarcation of parish boundaries. The most famous parish boundary cross is that of Marsa, which now stands some metres away from the original cross site. It is considered to be a landmark and was known as '*Croce Marsa*' or '*Is-Salib tal-Marsa*' ('The Marsa Cross'). This cross marks the split of the Valletta parish from the mother parish of Qormi. It also marks the boundaries between Valletta, Qormi and Tarxien. A strange event took place next to this cross. During the early 20th century a Maltese priest, Fr George Preca, was working hard to establish doctrine centres in all parishes. While he was walking from Ħamrun to the south of Malta, he had to pass by the Marsa Stone Cross. At that point he heard a voice and had a vision of a small boy pulling a cart full of dirt. The boy asked the priest to give him a hand. This vision had a special meaning for Fr Preca. He realised God was willing him to establish a lay teaching society and set up a doctrine centre in every parish. He succeeded in so doing, and nowadays, Fr Preca has been canonised as a saint.

Another famous landmark is *Is-Salib tal-Imrieħel* (The Mrieħel Cross). This cross stands on the spot where the parishes of Attard, Balzan and Birkirkara meet. According to a local tradition, this cross also marks the boundary between the two rival authorities, those of Mdina and Valletta. Any incident occurring north of this cross fell under the jurisdiction of Mdina while if it happened south of this cross it came under that of the Valletta authorities.

Stone crosses are also a typical characteristic of Malta. In former days they were more numerous but some had to be demolished due to an increase in traffic.

Stone cross and church dome, Mqabba.

Coastal towers

Many years ago, corsair landings in Malta used to occur quite often. In the 14th and 15th centuries, the waters around Malta were full of pirates. These used to sail in Maltese coves disembarking pirates who would land, pillage, as well as plunder the countryside. Many Maltese were taken into slavery while others were killed by these merciless pirates. Farmhouses were burnt, while animals, water and food were stolen. The Knights started thinking of making the north countryside safer. Their solution consisted of the erection of watchtowers around the coast. These towers were just outposts which sounded the alarm when an invasion or a pirate landing was imminent.

Watchtowers were not introduced by the Knights, however. On the site of Fort St Elmo, a watchtower built in 1488 already existed. Its function was to protect the Grand Harbour. This was dismantled to pave the way for the erection of Fort St Elmo. This fortress was built by the Knights in 1552 together with another fort, Fort St Michael in Senglea. After the Great Siege of 1565, pirate incursions continued.

It was Grand Master Alof de Wignacourt who ordered the construction of four towers. These were: San Luciano Tower at Marsaxlokk; San Tumas at Marsaskala (known also as 'Wied il-Għajn'); Wignacourt Tower or St Paul's Bay Tower at St Paul's Bay; and Torre Xgħajra (Xgħajra Tower) or *Santa Maria delle Grazie* Tower (Our Lady of Graces Tower) in Xgħajra, a locality near Żabbar. These watchtowers are large enough to be referred to as castles in some cases as they had a drawbridge which was drawn over a moat. These towers were quite strong and they definitely made it safer to live and work in their coastal areas.

It is worthwhile to mention that the oldest surviving tower on the Maltese islands built by the Knights is that of St Paul's Bay. It was designed by Vittorio Cassar, a Maltese architect and a military engineer of the Order of St John. It has a two-storey

Għajn Tuffieħa tower built by Grand Master Lascaris.

square structure and two barrel-vaulted chambers within. Its four corner towers served as look-out posts over both the countryside and the bay.

Grand Master Jean Paul de Lascaris Castellar continued on the work of Grand Master Alof de Wignacourt by commissioning the construction of another five watchtowers. The landing of corsairs was still onging and the Maltese still felt unsafe to live in the northern parts of the island. When Fra Martin de Redin was elected to the post of Grand Master, he decided to build a set of 13 watchtowers at strategic distances around the coast. These towers were built within sight of each other. The only part of the Maltese coast which was not covered by the de Redin plans of coastal watchtowers were the cliffs in the Siġġiewi and Dingli areas. It was considered that in this part of Malta no towers were needed since the high coastland offered was enough protection from pirates' landings.

St Agatha tower (also known as the red tower) overlooks Mellieħa bay.

The de Redin towers were built strongly and were compact in size. They consisted of a ground floor space surrounded by very strong walls. There was another room on the first floor which was reached by means of an outside ladder which was drawn up in case of a landing. These towers included a rock-cut cistern. They were manned morning and night. When the soldiers stationed at the watchtowers caught sight of any landing they used flags to communicate with each other. During the night a bonfire was lit. These signals passed from one tower to another until they reached the headquarters. Then, military preparations were made to face the landing pirates.

Other watchtowers were also erected in the interior of the island by the Maltese nobles and elite. These were larger than the de Redin coastal towers. Their façades were more elaborate. A case in point is *Torre Gauci* (Gauci Tower) which is located at San Pawl tat-Tarġa, a district of Naxxar. Qrendi has *Torre Cavalier* (the Knight's Tower) and Wied Żnuber has another such tower. A characteristic of these noble towers are the stone drop-boxes which are also referred to as 'machicolation'. These were used when the pirates were within reach of the tower.

A special noble tower was built at Marsaskala. This is referred to as '*Torri Mamo*' ('Mamo's Tower'). This tower was not planned in the form of a square, but rather, in the shape of the St Andrew cross. Its four extreme walls are very strong. Another noble fortified 'house'– Selmun Castle – was built in 1786 by Domenico Cachia, on Mellieħa ridge. It was designed according to the fashion of contemporary European fortified villas. It incorporated an imposting hall, a large banqueting room and bastioned turrets.

Grand Master Huges Loubenx de Verdalle built his fortified summer palace in the Boschetto ('little forest') area of Rabat. The plan was made by Girolamo Cassar in 1586. It is three storeys high and at its corners are bastioned towers. As these towers are higher than the castle itself, their roofs were used for signalling to the Magistral Palace in Valletta in case of enemy attack.

Gozo also had its noble interior tower: the former 7th-century Gourgion Tower. It included many stone drop-boxes, as well as heraldic shields and a slender domed staircase tower. This unique and historical tower was dismantled during the Second World War as a temporary landing ground was needed for aircrafts. Its stones were saved but the tower has not yet been rebuilt. Comino also had its own watchtower, built on a steep slope in 1618. This is *it-Torri ta' Santa Marija* (St Mary's Tower) which provided security for the strait waters between Malta and Comino, as well as those between Comino and Gozo. This tower was built thanks to the generosity of Grand Master Alof de Wignacourt. Its walls are about five metres thick and its barrel-vaulted chambers could house about 200 soldiers. After the French invasion in 1798, it was used by General Bonaparte's soldiers and later, by the Maltese resistance movement, the British and the Armed Forces of Malta.

Another historical defence building, which is considered to be part and parcel of the coastal tower system is *il-Knisja ta' San Girgor* (the Church of St Gregory) at Żejtun. This church has defence features. From its roof, signals used to be relayed to Mdina, the ancient capital, to alert the authorities that there was an attack or that a landing had taken place. During the daytime, these signals consisted of smoke, while bonfires were lit by night. On the roof of the church there was a stone trough in which the bonfires were lit.

By time, the coastal watchtowers became part and parcel of the Maltese environment. Some were given popular names. Among these we find a de Redin tower which is known as *it-Torri l-Abjad* (the White Tower) and another one known as *it-Torri l-Aħmar* (the Red Tower).

Built in 1618, St Mary's Tower dominates the high ground in Comino.

Xlendi tower in Munxar, Gozo, guards the entrance to Xlendi bay.

Overlooking the beautiful valley of Imtaħleb, the church of the Nativity of the Virgin serves the surrounding rural community.

The Houses and Dress

The Maltese Clock (*L-Arloġġ tal-Lira*)

It is believed that it was Grand Master Manoel Pinto de Fonseca (1741–73), a Portuguese, who introduced the Maltese to clock making. He wanted a special clock to decorate one of the magisterial palace courtyards, so he employed a clockmaker surnamed Clerici for this purpose. This clock was affixed on a turret on one side of the courtyard, where its gongs could be heard from every part of Valletta. The clock has four dials: one showing the time, the other the phase of the moon; the left dial denotes the month, while the right one registers the date. It is decorated by four bronze figures representing Moorish slaves holding hammers. The central figures are larger than the side ones.

The Maltese were carried away by the sound of the strikes of this clock, which filled the air around the palace. A small replica of this clock is found in the sacristy of the parish church of the Annunciation at Balzan.

After the introduction of the palace courtyard clock, clocks started to become popular with the Maltese. Many middle class Maltese and members of the aristocracy started planning to have a clock in their houses while the clergy wanted a clock

A typical Maltese clock hanging in an old workshop in Valletta.

Ditta Darmanin in St Paul's Street, Valletta, specialize in Maltese clocks.

for the parish church sacristy or parish priest's office. This created a demand for clocks, which led to the introduction of clock making in Malta. Three types of clocks started to be produced locally. There was the church clock fixed to the church's façade, adorning one of the belfries, as well as the mantelpiece or *gradenza* (chest of drawers) clock which also started to be made locally. The latter was popular with both the clergy and the middle class. Finally, there was the wall-hanging clock know as '*l-arloġġ tal-Lira*' or the 'Maltese clock'. Later, in the middle of the 19th century, the grandfather clock was also introduced to the local market.

The most popular clock was *l-arloġġ tal-Lira* (literally, 'the one Lira clock'), which reached Maltese homes in the 18th century. It was a time when the art scene in Malta was dominated by the French artist, Antoine de Favray. This painter produced many works of art showing Maltese house interiors, some of which include the Maltese clock.

According to tradition, this clock's name originated from the cost of its commission. Others disagree. They argue that in the past, it was a custom among the upper classes to present a wedding gift to a maid-servant who was about to get married and leave her job. The master of the house would call the maid-servant, thank her for her services, and ask her whether she would prefer a Maltese clock or a gold coin worth one pound (British sterling) as a present. Leading folklore scholar, Giovanni Bonello, suggests on the other hand that the phrase '*tal-lira*' derives from the word for 'lyre', which is pronounced like the Maltese word 'lira'.

In order to produce the Maltese clock, many craftsmen have to co-ordinate their services together. The carpenter prepares the red deal box; the clockmaker manufactures the clock machine; the artist paints the clock's façade scene; and the gilder finishes the precious ornamentation in gold leaf. It is of little wonder that this clock is the most sought after class of Maltese painted and gilded furniture. At first, the mechanism used to be made of wood but with the introduction of steel to the local market, clock making made a great step forward and timekeeping improved.

The Maltese clock consists of a decorative wooden box with a Roman numeral dial. In the centre of this dial there is usually a scene depicting the Grand Harbour or some floral design. If the clock is commissioned, it is traditional to have the family coat of arms painted in the upper part of the frame. Sometimes, the upper part shows the coat of arms of a grand master. The Maltese clock comes in different colours, the most popular being red, green, and black.

Nowadays, only a few craftsmen produce this type of clock. In the seventies, one of the local firms produced a number of copies of this clock in a red or green colour. They were genuine replicas of the original. As these clocks are considered to be typically Maltese, some local manufactures are producing small copies of them with battery driven machine.

The Coffer (*Is-Senduq*)

One of the characteristics of Maltese furniture is the coffer (*is-senduq*; plural *sniedaq*). This is a rectangular box, generally made of chestnut wood. Sometimes, any hard wood was used instead.

The Maltese coffer is a plain chest with short legs to raise it from the floor. Its dual purposes were of a depository for a daughter's dowry and a safe box for the family's gold and silver valuables. Sometimes family documents such as a commercial agreement for the purchase of arable land or property were also kept in the coffer. Marriage contracts treasured by the family members were also kept here. Some believe that the *senduq* was introduced in Malta during the Aghlabid period in the latter half of the 9th century. Its popularity spread to many parts of the Mediterranean and on the European continent.

The coffer was an integral part of the house's main room's furniture.

In former days, the coffer had other functions. It served as a seater during a family reunion. It offered storage space for clothes and furnishing when these were not in use. It could also be turned into a table or a bed for the head of the family.

By time, the coffer's use was taken over by the chest of drawers. It left the bedroom and became an integral part of the hall or the house's main room's furniture. In this new location, yellow or red brass or pieces of pottery started to decorate tops of coffers. This change in location also led the coffer to become more decorative. Domestic or historical scenes started to be carved on the side panels. The most common scenes were galleys of the Order of St John and harbour fortifications. Sometimes the legs of the coffer were made in the shape of a lion's paws. Coffers became popular again with the Maltese and many carpenters started producing solely coffers. A case in point is a family surnamed Camilleri at Żejtun, nicknamed '*Tas-Senduq*' ('of the coffer') by the locals.

In former days, the coffer included a miniature coffer to be placed inside it. This was meant for an infant daughter's future belongings. Her parents would start to invest in items such as clothing and linen from an early age for her dowry. This small coffer was also used to store jewels, gold and silver coins. Coinage, in the absence of banks, was used by the Maltese as a means of investment. All the Order and British gold coins were collectables and kept as part of the family wealth.

The coffer became part and parcel of the Maltese linguistic heritage. A proverb states that '*Aħjar ħabib is-suq milli mitt skut fis-senduq*' ('it is better to have a friend in the market-place than one hundred scudi in the coffer'). Moreover, we have an expression linking the coffer with one's possessions: '*Ta' fuqek senduqek*' ('what you're wearing is all you own', referring to someone who is poor).

Today the coffer is regarded as a precious piece of furniture, an item to be cherished.

The Chest of Drawers (*Il-Gradenza*)

In the 7th century, Malta was ruled by the Knights of St John. Many knights resided in Malta and they brought their traditions as well as the novelties which had become popular in their country of origin. During this period, the coffer (*senduq*) became unpopular with the knights and members of the aristocracy. Some coffer designers started to create hall benches. The younger generation started to prefer a chest of drawers (*gradenza*) to the coffer. The Maltese carpenter started to produce this type of furniture for which demand was ever growing. Several types and different sizes of Maltese chests of drawers were made. The smaller type were known as '*gradenzini*'.

There are four types of *gradenzi*. The most popular was that known as '*Tal-Maqrut*'. This chest can be distinguished by its serpentine shape. Many Maltese antique lovers refer to it as 'truly Maltese'. Genuine replicas continued to be made in some quarters of Valletta until the late 1970s. The second type – a small chest of drawers – is known as '*Tal-Qassis*', meaning 'belonging to the priest'. The third is known as '*Tal-Għarusa*' – 'belonging to the bride'– and contained the bride's outfit and jewellery, as well as her dowry of gold and silver pieces. The fourth type was known as '*Tal-Iljun*' ('of the lion') as it had lion paws for legs and grotesque lion face motifs.

The demand for chests of drawers made Maltese carpenters look at continental styles for inspiration. This probably happened when someone would have imported a chest of drawers from Europe or obtained one from a member of the Order and commissioned a replica. Maltese carpenters seem to have been well prepared for this new type of furniture as today's antique lovers and dealers find it difficult to distinguish whether a particular piece of furniture was actually made in Malta or somewhere else in Europe. The most popular styles were similar to those of Naples and Sicily. People in the antique

A Maltese-17th-century chest of drawers.

trade try to examine the chest of drawers and look for three clues to establish whether it was manufactured locally or not. The clues are splintering backs, crude drawer interiors, and the way iron locks are fitted to the chest. The Maltese carpenters preferred to place the iron lock over the wood rather than inserting it inside the wood.

Chests of drawers were made in solid or veneered walnut. Sometimes mahogany was used. They were decorated with inlaid patterns, the most popular being the Maltese eight-pointed cross. Sometimes, the cross was replaced by a multi-pointed star or a floral design.

Working families had their chests of drawers too. These were made of simple wood and their tops were decorated with devotional items such as holy pictures, photos of deceased members of the family, and a statue of either their patron saint or the locality's titular saint. Candles or oil lamps were lit during the night in front of these sacred images.

By time, chests of drawers moved rooms. At first, they used to be placed in bedrooms, making it easier for the resident to take the clothes which he or she was about to wear. As demand increased, these pieces of furniture became more and more elaborate, and were then placed in the main public areas of the house or palace – the hall, the lounge or the dining area.

When the chest of drawers was kept in the bedroom, on its top were placed artistic and religious objects. These objects made it necessary for the carpenter to cover the top with marble. When the *gradenza* left the bedroom, these chests of drawers started to be decorated with a gilded mirror, a painting or a Maltese clock hanging on the wall above it. Thus, there was no more use for a marble top.

Nowadays, on the surface of the chest one finds lace doilies with a mantle piece clock or a *gradenza* clock on top. Sometimes, these items are flanked by a pair of alabaster vases. Alternatively, a porcelain vase is placed against a set of silver-framed photos. These chests of drawers are usually inherited from one generation to another and are seldom put up for sale in an auction.

The Balcony (*Il-Gallarija*)

All types of buildings with two storeys or more, from the greatest palaces to the humblest of houses, include a balcony. Some are of the opinion that it was the Arabs who introduced balconies in Malta. Others believe that the machicolations of the Holy Land influenced the Maltese to introduce balconies on the façades of their houses. Examples of these types of balconies can still be found in the towers of San Pawl tat-Tarġa at Naxxar and an octagonal tower in Qrendi.

Usually, the balconies are made by building a stone shelf which is called a '*soprabank*'. This shelf rests on two or more corbelled supports called '*saljaturi*', some of which are plain and some heavily carved. Timber, stone, or wrought iron structures are placed on top of the stone shelf to complete the balcony. Some balconies had little peep-holes to enable the resident to see who was at the door without being seen.

There are three types of balconies in Malta. The stone type are the oldest. Some historians believe that these balconies were simply an addition to the stone parapet. At first, stone balconies were produced with plain panels, but by time, these started to be carved with various designs, the most popular being the eight-pointed cross, a symbol which the Maltese islands inherited from the Knights of St John. Sometimes, a recessed shell (*arzella*) enclosed the balcony doorway to accompany the stone balcony design. Balzan has a heavily carved balcony in its village core, while the villages of Gozo – including Għarb, San Lawrenz and Rabat – can all boast of

A decorated limestone balcony, Gozo.

An ornate wooden balcony in St Ursola Street, Valletta.

a large patrimony of carved stone balconies. These are open balconies, with no canopy to provide shade or protection from weather conditions. In the baroque period, the stone panels of open balconies were replaced by balusters. These balusters became very popular and soon they started to appear also on top of roofs.

Similar to the stone balconies we find wrought iron balconies. The only difference is that these have iron panels instead of stone ones. Wrought iron panels were heavily decorated and were mostly manufactured at Naxxar. By time, the main door and the ground floor openings started to include a small window to lighten up the room. These were protected by wrought iron panels. The designs of the balcony panels, the stairs railings, and the window and main door openings had similar panel designs, and they were truly works of art.

Finally, there are the timber balconies. These are closed balconies with glass which offer protection from weather conditions. They can also serve as extra space for the family, such as, for example, a children's play area. The standard Maltese timber balcony has three to four glass 'windows' in the front, and one on each side. The bottom panels are usually made of solid wood with no openings at all. Some historians believe that timber balconies were introduced by the Knights of St John. According to Bosio's history book (published in 1602) about the Order, the aerial drawing of Valletta does not depict any building having a timber box-shaped balcony. It is believed that the first closed timber balcony was made around 1679 to cover the corner balconies of the Order's main palace – the Palace of the Grand Master (today's Presidential Palace) in Valletta. These timber and glass structures had the purpose of joining the rooms on the sides of the Palace.

A closed balcony with an adjacent timber-floored counterpart.

A block furnished with neatly stacked balconies, Valletta.

During the 18th century, this type of balcony became very popular with the Maltese and it spread from Valletta to the villages where it became fashionable and replaced the open stone or wrought-iron balconies.

The Maltese timber balconies used to be painted in green or beige. By time, the main door and the timber windows were also painted in the same colour. Nowadays, this tradition is being challenged and all the colours of the rainbow are being used. In the old villages one can notice small metal lugs on the façades of timber balconies. These used to be made to hold wrought iron brackets for little oil lamps. These lamps were lit on feast days, especially while the titular or Good Friday processions were passing through the street. In the 20th century, these lamps were also lit on Christmas Eve while the Christmas Eve procession was passing by on its way to the parish church for the Christmas Eve Children's service. Today, these oil lamps have been replaced by electric bulbs.

Occasionally, one might come across a timber floored balcony. These balconies have a different history to narrate. Originally, they were windows which were enlarged by eliminating the bottom layers of stone. A timber floor was then created and supported by wrought iron brackets.

Balconies are still popular with the Maltese to this day. They are usually made of concrete with aluminium frames. Sometimes, these modern big balconies are made in such a way as to provide more physical space and light to the room.

In former days, balconies were especially popular with Maltese women. In the absence of television, after running errands and doing housework, they used to spend their free time on a high stool watching the world go by in the street. It was the only means for them to get the latest parish or village news, as women had no bars to frequent as their male counterparts did. This custom is still strong in the small villages and on the island of Gozo.

Lace (*Il-Bizzilla*)

Pillow lace was created in the Italian city of Genoa in the 16th century. By time, its demand increased and lacemaking spread throughout Europe. Lace was introduced in Malta by members of the Order of St John. Some are of the opinion that around 1640, pillow lace started to be manufactured locally. Due to demand by the knights, the clergy and the members of the Maltese aristocracy, lacemakers increased. It continued to flourish until the end of the 18th century, when the islands were taken over by Napoleon Bonaparte. During the French occupation, lacemaking almost died out. The craft was revived by Lady Hamilton Chichester, who took great interest in Maltese lace and did her utmost to revive pillow lacemaking.

During the 19th century, a piece of lace was given to Marjana Attard, a Gozitan woman, by a member of the clergy, Fr Ġwann Curmi. The woman was completely swept away by this piece of lace and started to copy its pattern. She managed to produce lace and then passed her 'discovery' on to her sister as well as to other friends. The skill of pillow lacemaking was born in Gozo and it became popular with Gozitan women and girls as well as with the Gozitan clergy, to enrich their sacred vestments and church furnishings. The Gozitans were not happy only to produce lace; they went a step further by starting to create new stitches such as the 'Mosche', a leaf-shaped design.

The lacemaker, detail from a painting by Antoine de Favray.

The demand for lace was so great that schools were opened in Victoria. The first school was run by Regina Rapa and her niece Baldomina, known as '*tal-Grieg*'. As demand continued to increase, another school, Casa Industriale, was opened in Xagħra by another member of the clergy, Fr Ġużepp Diacono, known as '*tal-Bambini*'. Fr Diacono was a very creative man and designed several geometric patterns which were worked in lace by the pupils of this Casa Industriale. He also opened another school in Gozo, this time in Rabat.

Fr Diacono also introduced black silk shawls. They became popular with both the Maltese ladies as well as with English ladies, who were on the islands to visit members of the family who worked in the British Services. These black silk shawls were a real money boosters and many Gozitan families increased their family income as a result.

Lace is made on a pillow which is locally known as '*trajbu*'. This pillow is made up of bundle of dry straw stalks. Each *trajbu* is about 60 centimetres long. The bundle is then wrapped up in a piece of hessian cloth and sewn up very tightly. The next step is the covering of the lace pillow with cotton, several sheets of newspaper, and flour paste. The lace pillow is then left in the direct rays of the sun to dry. It is finally covered in strong brown paper.

When the *trajbu* is ready the pattern is pinned to the upper end the lace thread is then woven around the pins. This has a dual function: the basic pattern is produced, and both the pattern and the lace could be placed on the lace pillow. The lacemaker starts filling up the bobbins, which are usually made of fruit tree wood with thread. We find different types of bobbins, but the most popular with lacemakers is the dark type. It is worthwhile to mention that in former days bobbins were also made of bone. Bone bobbins became unpopular with the lacemakers as they tended to wear out more quickly.

Lacemaking in Malta and Gozo traces its origins back to the 16th century.

We find different types of threads used in lacemaking in Malta. Some use silk and others use fine linen. Sometimes, coarser threads are also used. The thread is wound around the upper part of the bobbin. This method helps the lacemaker to manipulate the thread better around the pins. The thread is even weighed down so that the thinner strand of lace becomes even in thinness.

In former days, Gozitan women used to take the *trajbu* and a chair out on the family's doorstep. They would invite other lacemakers to join them. They then sat there, placing one end of the *trajbu* on the lacemaker's lap and the other end against the wall of the house façade. While they worked, they chatted: all the village news was discussed together with novelties that roused their curiosity. During the 1960s, work became difficult and emigration became popular with Gozitan families. Many families settled in other parts of the British Commonwealth, such as Australia and Canada, as well as in the United States of America. Some women continued making lace in their new homeland and today, one can still meet with pieces of lace created by these women.

Queen Victoria is said to have bought Gozitan lace. In 1838, she is reputed to have ordered eight dozen pairs of long and another eight dozen pairs of short mitts, as well as a scarf. When Gozo was raised to the dignity of diocese, the Gozitans presented Pope Pius IX with a piece of Gozo lace. This was worked by the daughters of notary Franġisk Calleja. In former days, many Gozitan lacemakers had their agents in Malta. They used to sell them their products and in return, they would supply them with money and threads. When the Grand Harbour was hosting a Royal Navy warship, the agents used to go to the harbour, embark on a boat, and try to sell the lace pieces to the members of the crew on the warships. There were also specialised Valletta shops that sold only lace pieces. Nowadays, many Maltese households buy lace to serve as doilies and tablecloths. Some women also like a white or a black scarf or shawl.

Lacemaking was one of Bedfordshire's (England) main industries. In 1768, there were some 500 women and girls working in the lace industry. By the 1830s, the industry was in decline. A leading Bedford lace dealer called Thomas (Thomazin) Lester and his sons tried to revive this industry. During the 1850s they introduced a new type of lace which was inspired by Gozo lace. It became known as the 'Bedfordshire Maltese lace'. It became popular with lacemakers as it was simpler, quicker and easier to produce. Prizes were also won by

Lacemaking in the island of Gozo *c.*1939.

these English lacemakers during exhibitions held in London, Vienna and Chicago. Samples of the Bedfordshire Maltese lace are on display at the Cecil Ghiggins art gallery and museum at Castle Close in Bedford.

Gozo lace has several typical patterns, which have been influenced by different international sources, from the East, Portugal and Spain, to Italy and France.

The Gozo lace has its own characteristics. It is famous for four different motifs: the Maltese cross (*is-Salib tal-Kavallieri*); the star (*il-festun tal-istilla*); the flower (*il-festun tal-warda*); and the flower and raised work border. There are also characteristic stitches: the whole stitch (*it-tila*); the edging (*il-puntina*); net stitch (*il-fillieri*); trellis stitch (*il-kannizzata*); whole stitch with net stitch (*it-tila mal-fillieri*); spider stitch (*il-brimba*); the leaf stitch (*il-moska*); the raised work (*il-moska fuq it-torxon*); the fan stitch (*l-imrewħa*); chevon square pattern; the English stitch (*il-punt Ingliż*); the boll stitch (*il-punt tal-balla*); rose ground (*il-punt tal-kaxxi*); half stitch (*in-nofs punt*); and the Picot stitch (*il-punt fuq il-labra*).

Many churches, convents and monasteries have their collections of sacred vestments which include Maltese lace. It is a common practice for church sextons to include a white rectangular altar cloth (*terħa*) edged with locally produced lace. Some of these altar furnishings include special motifs and patterns, while others include the symbols of the Holy Eucharist or the pelican and ears of corn. All the Maltese Carmelite convents can boast of a very interesting collection of sacred vestments enriched with locally produced lace. They are indeed works of art.

The Maltese cross is characteristic of Gozo lace.

The Door Knockers (*Il-Ħabbata*)

Old Maltese houses used to equip the main door with a mechanical doorbell. This consisted of a handle attached to a wire which was further attached to a coiled spring that shook the bell when pulled. A further piece of equipment for the main door was a mud iron scraper embedded in the ground. The purpose of this scraper was for anyone entering the house to scrape mud off their shoes before proceeding inside. Some iron mud scrapers were made in the form of an animal, the most popular being a dog.

While visiting the core of an old village one would notice that, apart from the bell and iron mud-scraper, every townhouse or middle class dwelling door had a ceramic or metal knob, or a brass door knocker on each of its two wings. The knobs helped the resident to either open or close the door wing more easily. Sometimes, instead of the door knobs, one could find a pair of door knockers. These knockers gave a more elegant look to the main door, making it more stately. Usually these knockers reflected the status of the head of the family who lived within the walls of the particular house.

In Malta, there are different types of knockers. The traditional type consists of a ball or boss with holes at the sides from which a heavy semi-circular ring hangs. Usually, in the middle of this ring, is a small ball which hits against a round boss fixed to the door at a lower level. These types of knockers – often coloured black – can be found on all types of urban or rural buildings, and even farmhouses. As these were popular, they were made by local craftsmen, especially those of Naxxar.

By time, more elaborate knockers were imported. Sometimes, the knocker ball was transformed into the head of a slave; sometimes, a lion. Both the slave- and the lion-shaped balls had holes in their faces from which a semi-circular ring hung. Other types consisted of a plain ball with the semi-circular ring

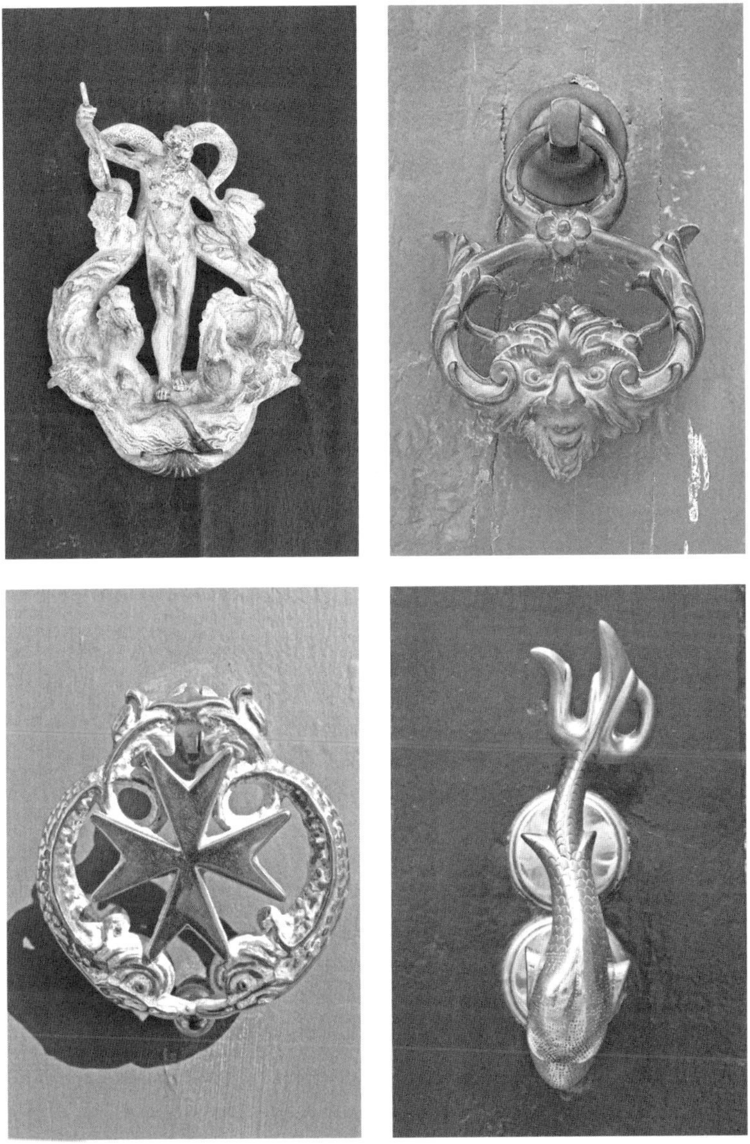

Maltese door knockers come in all shapes and forms.

Large baroque door knockers fixed to enormous main doors.

being replaced by a pair of hands decorated with shirt lace or even a ring. This hand would be made to hold a ball among the fingers which knocked against the door ball. The dolphin is yet another common type of door knocker. Inside the semi-circular ring a brass figure of this mammal would be set with its tail at the top and its mouth at the far end. The head of the dolphin would be used to hit the lower door ball. We find two types of dolphin knockers: the smooth-skinned or the scaly types. Both the hands and the dolphins were manufactured in Malta by a local factory which opened its doors after the Second World War.

The upper classes and the members of the aristocracy had large baroque door knockers fixed to their enormous main doors. These consisted of two small children holding a coat of arms. These family shields did not belong to the Maltese noble families, as the knockers were imported rather than being made locally. From time to time, styles varied. Between the wars, the vanity style reached Malta, and there were townhouses and noble palaces which had adopted this style.

When a person was at the door, he or she would hold one of the knockers in their hand, raise it and then let it go against the lower ball part. Usually, this occurred twice. This created a thudding sound which would summon the resident to the door. If no one appeared at the door, the neighbours would often show up and inform the visitor whether the residents were fast asleep or away on an errand.

Door knockers served another function. They advertised the level of cleanliness of the maid of the house. These were cleaned after washing the two wings of the door and the door steps. They were the last item to be attended to. The shinier they were, the better. The maids of the village townhouses used to vie with each other about this. Highly polished brass knockers were the talk of the towns people. Polishing was usually done on Saturdays before the maid left the household to spend the weekend with her family.

The Maltese Farmhouse (*Ir-Razzett*)

Scattered all over the Maltese islands, we find various farmhouses (popularly known as *'ir-razzett'*, plural *'l-irziezet'*). We find these dwellings either in the open countryside or clustered together outside village cores. The open countryside farmhouses are encircled by patches of fields enclosed by dry stone walls (*il-ħitan tas-sejjieħ*), surrounded by prickly pears and carob trees.

According to some researchers interested in architecture, these dwellings were influenced by the Arabs. But Anthony Luttrell has a different opinion. He thinks that the Maltese farmhouses with their courtyard plans could have been influenced either by Roman or Sicilian countryside buildings. These buildings, which were erected by countrymen, had to meet several purposes. They had to offer shelter as well as security to the farmer and his family. They also had to accommodate the rearing of animals, that is, they had to provide space for the safe-keeping of animals during the dark hours of the night and offer storage space for the animals' food. The walls had to be ideal for the Mediterranean climate, with its long, hot, dry summers and short, cold, windy, winter days. The stone used was that offered by the geology of the Maltese archipelago, that is, limestone (*franka*).

History had a great influence on these dwellings. During the Medieval and the Knights' times, landings by corsairs were common and frequent. This entailed that farmhouses should be built inland rather than along the coast. Most of these dwellings were erected in the centre or south of the island of Malta. Usually, they were built in some narrow or meandering alley next to a settlement and fields. Sometimes, three or four farmhouses were built next to each other forming a little community, or around a small square where the farmers' families could come together and help each other in times of need. The few which were built close to the sea were usually built on hilltop sites so that the farmer and his family felt protected from sudden attacks.

To make farmhouses safe, their façades did not include windows. All external openings were small and all the rooms had their openings giving onto an internal, central yard. Moreover, the only opening for entering the farmhouse was covered by a bare, thick, wooden door, which also opened onto a sunny central courtyard. The walls were quite thick and usually consisted of an outer and an inner stone facing. The space between these facings was usually filled in with stone chippings and soil.

The 'code of practice' for erecting a farmhouse was simple but effective. Naturally, it reflected the lifestyle of those times.

A Maltese farmhouse overlooking St Paul's Islands.

The first step was taken by the farmer, who faced the need to have a farmhouse for the family. After making up his mind he would choose a site, usually next to the fields either owned by or hired to the family. He would then call some men who had some experience in constructing farmhouses or, if these were not available, he would call on some friends or members of the extended family. Work on the new farmhouse would then start and those involved were usually paid in kind.

A typical farmhouse consisted of a two-storey building. The rooms on the ground floor were used by domestic animals. The most common animals would be a donkey or a mule, some cows, poultry, sheep and a good number of goats. If the farmer had pigs, these were usually placed in separate quarters in a small building outside the farmhouse proper.

The rooms on the upper floor were planned for the family. The upper floor was reached by means of a small flight of steps

A farmhouse in the limits of Rabat.

built inside the courtyard. If the farmhouse was a large one, all the upper rooms were joined by means of an open-sheltered corridor resembling a long verandah. Usually, this passage included arched openings overlooking the courtyard.

The rooms were often long and narrow. Their high ceilings were made of long ceiling slabs (*xorok*). These slabs were supported either by wooden beams or stone arches. The floor was always lined with stone slabs.

A Maltese farmhouse has its typical characteristics. The entrance door, which is usually arched, is wide enough to allow a cart to pass through it. This door either leads to a central courtyard or to the ground floor rooms, which were usually used as stables. Next to the door we find two architectural features where domestic animals, such as a donkey, horse or mule, could be tied. The most common would be a semi-circular stone projecting from the façade wall. A rope could be passed through a hole in the stone for tethering an animal. If the façade did not include this circular stone, or if this was broken, the farmer would drill two holes in a slanting direction into the wall. These holes converged into each other to form a V-shaped tunnel to enable the farmer to pass the rope and tie up his animal.

Next to the door we find stone sockets which once supported the wooden door or gate. Sometimes, the ground floor rooms have rectangular openings for light and air. These openings could be closed from the inside by means of a piece of stone. Windows were only built on the first floor – the living quarters of the farmer's family. A small window was usually built in each of the upper floor rooms. One of these windows often has a pair of stone brackets just below its ledge on the outside wall. In former days a stone slab was placed on these brackets to support a plant of sweet basil, carnations or rosebush, to announce that the family had a daughter of marriageable age.

Semi-circular projecting stone used to pass a rope for tethering animals.

The roof of the farmhouse is flat like that of all the other Maltese dwellings. This area serves as a catchment for rainwater which is collected in a cistern dug out of rock below the courtyard. This water used to meet the needs of all the family and the animals of the particular farmhouse. Traditionally, the farmer slipped an eel or two in this cistern as these creatures were believed to purify the water.

Some farmhouses include a dovecote with squarish apertures on one of the courtyard's walls, in which the doves could build their nests and rear their young. Other farmhouses feature a stone sundial. If the farmhouse is located in a cluster of other similar dwellings, the façade could easily be decorated with a recessed niche with sacred images of Jesus Christ, His Mother, or some saints. Some farmhouses, which were built by the Grand Masters, other prominent members of the Order, or members of the Maltese aristocracy, bear a sculptured coat of arms over the door. These farmhouses were built during the times of the Knights, when every building was adorned with the family coat of arms.

Today, farmhouses are highly sought after by both the Maltese and foreign settlers. The latter are mainly pensioners who come to Malta to spend the rest of their days in a carefree atmosphere. Some farmhouses have been modernised to make them suitable for modern living. Some even include a swimming pool to freshen up during the long, hot, dry summer days.

Converted farmhouses with pools offer both charm and comfort.

The Windmill (*Il-Mitħna*)

In the outskirits of some villages, one can still come across a windmill (*il-mitħna*) or part of such a building. Windmills were introduced before the arrival of the Knights in 1530. When Grand Master Philippe Villiers de l'Isle Adam was considering taking over the archipelago of Malta and the African city of Tripoli as the Knights' independent home, he sent a Commission on behalf of the Order, to prepare a report about the social and economic conditions of Malta. In this report, we come across reference to windmills.

When the Knights set foot in Malta, they made sure to create a monopoly on the construction of windmills. By time, they owned all the windmills available on the Islands. Seldom did they sell any windmills or else give permission to the local people to build one. The knights set up foundations by which windmills could be erected. This leasing generated money then used to finance various projects. Grand Masters Fra Jean Paul de Lascaris Castellar, Fra Nicolas Cotoner, and Fra Antonio Manoel de Vilhena all had their own foundations. It is worthwhile mentioning that the leasing rates in Gozo were higher than those in Malta. This was mainly because the Gozitan windmills used to be more productive then their Maltese counterparts.

In the early years of British Rule, there were about 26 windmills in Malta and five in Gozo, all in good working condition. After 1838 the Government monopoly on windmills was lifted and anyone interested in doing so was allowed to build a windmill. Windmills lost their importance at the beginning of the 20th century when steam mills were introduced to the islands. These were first built around the Grand Harbour area. It seems that windmills kept functioning until the eve of the Second World War. A case in point is a windmill in Żejtun which stayed in operation until 1939.

Xarolla windmill dating back to 1724 and St Andrew's chapel in Żurrieq.

The Knights gave great importance to windmills and silos, as there was always a shortage of wheat in Malta. Locally grown wheat was never enough to feed the entire population. This problem increased with the coming of the Knights and their 'entourage', which included servants, slaves, soldiers and attendants. To make matters worse, many Rhodean families, whose livelihood depended on the Knights, decided to face exile with them. They left Rhodes in 1522 and settled in Malta too. To solve this age old problem, in the late Middle Ages, Malta had started to import grain from Sicily. At the time, since Malta formed part of the Kingdom of Sicily, it also had the right to buy this commodity without paying the export tax. The Knights worked hard to extend this privilege.

In order to store grain, the Knights built granaries (*il-fosos*). These were considered to be part and parcel of the system of defence, as these were seen as a protection against sieges and naval blockades. Valletta had 70 granaries built in hard rock in front of the Fort St Elmo. Castile Place was another locality

The granaries (here in Floriana) or *fossos* are bell-shaped reservoirs, each covered with a large stone cap, carefully sealed with mortar when full of wheat.

in Valletta, which included granaries with 15 of them in front of the Auberge de Castille. Floriana had the largest amount of granaries. These were built in front of the parish church in a square which bears their name to this day, Granaries Square. This is also the largest square in Malta. It was Grand Master Fra Gregorio Carafa who thought of building more granaries on the other side of the Grand Harbour. He built about 24 of these in Senglea and Birgu.

Maltese windmills have their particular characteristics. They are located outside the built-up area of the villages, on high land to make good use of the wind. The base of these windmills is usually squarish, but we find some that have a circular base. A windmill at Lija is a case in point, while we also find another such windmill at Qala, Gozo.

On entering a windmill, one finds an entrance hall with two rooms on both sides. Two of these rooms were used for storage, one for grain and the other for flour. Behind the hall comes the entrance to the windmill's tower (*it-tromba*). The upper part of the tower used to be made out of wood and is called '*kuppletta*' (a small dome). This area includes a circular flight of steps rising from the ground floor to the upper top opening. The rooms of the first floor used to serve as living quarters for the miller (*it-taħħan*) and his family. It was here that the miller's family had their kitchen, the dining room and the bedrooms. These rooms used to be furnished with traditional, countryside furniture. Sometimes, there would also be items which the miller's wife and daughters would use for weaving cloth and carpets, or producing lace and embroidered linen. In the kitchen one could then see the traditional utensils and working ware. Some windmills offered clients the possibility

The circular Tal-Qaret windmill in Żurrieq was built in 1674.

to bake bread. In this case the windmill would also incorporate an oven.

The tower normally includes two opposite facing doors, which enabled the miller to fix the sails which were needed for a particular working day. The windmill used to have six mill arms which were called *'artinni'*. Each arm had two sails, one was large and the other was small. These were linked to the grinding mill which used to be located at the bottom of the tower. The milling mechanism consisted of two big hard stones. The lower one was fixed, while the top stone could move in a circular motion thus crushing the grain placed between the stones. On the ground floor, the miller used to have his workshop, which housed a vast array of tools.

The daily lives of the people of both towns and villages was centred around the windmill. When the wind was favourable for the windmill to work, the miller would inform the local people by blowing a triton shell (*il-bronja*). Everyone would then bring their cereals to the miller. Here people met and while waiting for their flour, they discussed general affairs as well as circulating news and gossip. Sometimes, government enactments and proclamations were also read out here.

It seems that every windmill was built within sight of other neighbouring windmills. This made it possible for the miller to observe, from an opening in the upper part of his windmill tower, whether the other millers were at work or not. Some scholars argue that these windmills were part of a system of defence that operated a network of communication in case of any unwelcome landing or invasion by corsairs.

According to a report on windmills, Malta is considered to have the highest density of windmills in the world. Some localities had one or two windmills. Tarxien had two windmills in its village core. One was in Paola Road and another in Betta Street. The former windmill, which had Norman decorations, was replaced by a block of buildings while the latter one's base is being used as a store for the Annunciation feast outdoor decorations. Rabat in Malta had five windmills. These were located at Ħal Bajjada, Ta' Palajsa, Ta' Egħriexem, Taċ-Ċogħqi and Ta' Ħad-Dingli – all districts of Rabat.

Apart from the traditional windmills, Malta had smaller mills which were driven by horses or donkeys. These were called '*ċentimoli*'. These were introduced in Malta by V. Vogo, who was a resident of the Sicilian city of Palermo. There were also water mills called '*milendini*'.

Some windmills became famous. Żurrieq has a windmill which is well preserved and still has its own sails. This is situated between this village and that of Safi, in a district known as 'Tax-Xarolla'. Between Żabbar and Żejtun, there is another famous windmill known as '*Ta' Bir Għeliem*' or the Bulebel windmill ('*il-Mitħna ta' Bulebel*'). Bir Għeliem was a district which extended to Tarxien, covering the whole area around this windmill. Built at the beginning of the 1700s, it overlooked

This windmill in Mosta was converted into a private residence.

Another view of the restored Xarolla windmill in Żurrieq.

the fields surrounding this district. It stopped working in 1887. Nowadays, it lies on a large roundabout witnessing cars pass by in all directions. During the Second World War, this windmill was used to send signals to British bases in the area.

Another famous windmill is found at Birkirkara. It is known as *'il-Mitħna ta' Ganu'* ('Ganu's windmill'). It was built in 1724 during the reign of Grand Master Fra Antonio Manoel de Vilhena. Its detailed plan is found in a document called *'Cabreo o sia descrizione della Fondazione Manoel'*, housed in the National Library. This windmill kept working until 1929. After being neglected for many years it was then restored by the Public Works Department. It is presently being used as a modern art gallery by the renowned Maltese ceramicist and sculptor, Gabriel Caruana.

Another well-kept windmill is located at Xagħra in Gozo. This windmill is called *'Ta' Kola'* ('Nicholas's windmill') and dates back to 1725. It seems that the mason and his team used some bad quality stones and mortar to build this windmill. Because of this, an order was issued to dismantle it. It was then rebuilt in the 1780s. Its name originated from the Christian name of the last miller. He was Ġużeppi Grech who was popularly known as *'Żeppu ta' Kola'* (Joseph, son of Nicholas). This windmill still has its sails and is open to visitors. It contains a museum of objects which were used by a miller's family. There are tools linked to the milling trade as well as items found in domestic circles.

The Maltese House (*Id-Dar*)

Traditional village houses in Malta were at first inspired by the countryside farmhouses. On entering such houses, one finds a long room called *'l-intrata'* ('the hall') which leads to an open courtyard (*il-bitħa*). The rest of the house consists of rooms of different sizes which surround this courtyard. The courtyard contains a flight of steps which leads to a first floor room or two. The rest of the first floor consists of a rooftop. At the back of the house there might be a little garden with fruit trees.

After the Maltese and Knights' victory of the Great Siege of 1565, the Knights decided to construct a city–fortress which served their needs. Valletta started to be built. During those times, baroque concepts which had become popular in early 17th century in Italy, became desirable to the Knights. Several façades inside the city were given a decorative appearance to bring them in line with what was happening in Italy. Several main buildings such as the langues' small churches were all dressed up with baroque façades. Cases in point are the churches of St James, St Catherine and Our Lady of Pilar. Moreover, corners of building blocks had to be decorated with sculptural decorations, which also reflected this style.

Villa Marchese, Attard. Painting by Anton Schranz the elder (1769-1840).

After 1650, timber balconies were introduced in Valletta and these further enhanced the façades. These balconies were mostly made by a great number of Turkish slaves living in Malta at the time. They were master craftsmen in various trades, especially in carpentry. The balconies started to be decorated according to baroque designs inspired by the great Italian architects such as Borromini, Bernini and Cortona. The corbels (*saljaturi*) which support these balconies bear such flowery and decorative carvings.

Maltese architects and master masons got to know of this influence either by studying Italian buildings from books or by visiting the Eternal City of Rome. They also had the opportunity to study works of resident Italian architects who were in Malta working for the Knights. Architects such as

The flamboyant baroque windows of Casa Bolino, Valletta.

Blondel and Carapecchia all created buildings with baroque façades. Valletta could be compared to other contemporary towns in central Europe, such as Palmanova in North Italy.

The idea of a baroque house reached the towns and villages of Malta. The rooms of these houses have extremely high ceilings; slender stone slabs are perched on wooden beams or upheld by arches. Courtyards are spacious and staircases are charming. There is also a number of small rooms which were usually used as bedrooms. These rooms were easy to warm up on a cold winter's night. All these features give the Maltese house a special character.

These houses also incorporate a *kantina* (cellar). When the houses were built, the masons used to get the stone from the site itself. This not only offered free stones but was also in line with the Maltese belief that if stones were carried over a

An elegant 18th-century rococo staircase inside a Valletta palazzo.

long distance these would get offended and eventually lead to weathering problems. Thus, quarrying made it possible for the owner of the house to have a *kantina,* which also offered many advantages to the house. A system of grills from the *kantina* to the courtyard ensured that the house had enough ventilation. This kept the house cooler in the summer months and warmer in the winter days. Moreover, it prevented the rising of dampness inside the house, as well as providing a good storage place for the family's needs.

Not all baroque houses were large. A small baroque house would include a hall with sculptural decorations on the ceiling and walls. These decorations are mostly found around doors. The hall leads to a room which faces the house's front. This room used to be referred to as '*il-persjana*' (the 'louvred door') because its outer door consists of a large door with louvers in the upper part while the lower part is made from decorated solid wood. Both parts open onto the street. At the back of this louvred door we find a second door. Above the louvres, a small window opens towards the inside of the room. In the summer months, this window gives light and offers a means of ventilation. The external part of the *persjana* is traditionally painted in the same colour as the main door and the wooden balconies. The internal *persjana* door is always coloured bright white. This room used to serve as a sitting room with a wicker, five-piece suite or a Maltese sitting set with lion shaped legs and damask soft furnishing. Family portraits used to hang on the walls of this room. If the head of the house was a professional person he would also have a mahogany library or a desk inside this room.

After the hall one finds the *kontra-intrata* (second hall), which includes a flight of stairs. The stairs serve all the floors and end next to the roof. This area usually includes a coffer (*senduq*) or a round table with one strong leg at the centre. Along the stair walls there is usually a set of engravings showing the

The library inside Casa Rocca Piccola, a noble Maltese palazzo.

Grand Masters of Malta or some Valletta or village scenes. This area leads to another room which was used as a dining room. This furniture was traditionally made of solid mahogany and would contain the best dinner set and cutlery pieces. In one of the drawers there would also be a large linen tablecloth. Some silver items used to be exhibited inside the main showcase. Next, we find an arched and covered space overlooking the courtyard. This area served as a kitchen with a side table where all the cooking was done. The rest of this area was left space for a table and a set of chairs. A *gwardakarne* (a special cupboard for storing food) was also kept here.

The second floor consists of two or three rooms used as bedrooms. The main bedroom was called *'is-sala'*. In this large room one would find the bedroom suite of the couple. The furniture used to be made of solid mahogany. A holy picture

A typical Maltese townhouse, Siġġiewi.

usually depicting the Holy Family was hung over the bed. The furniture of the other bedrooms were usually made out of red deal. When drainage facilities were made available to the village dwellers, a small room was turned into a bathroom.

The rooftop was used for hanging out clothes to dry. These were washed in the courtyard during the summer months and inside the arched room or kitchen in winter. On the front side of the roof, a flag pole stand was often erected, usually featuring a sculptural work showing the symbols of the village or town's patron saint. The family who had a flag pole used to have a set of flags which were mainly: the white-and-red flag Maltese flag, the yellow-and-white Vatican flag (*'tal-Papa'*), and the red-and-white cross flag of the Order of St John (*'tal-fidi'* – *'of the faith'*). If the parish church was dedicated to the Blessed Virgin, the house owner would have another flag: a white-and-blue flag for Our Lady (*'tal-Madonna'*). Sometimes, a special flag was commissioned to be flown on the locality's feast day.

The facade of the Aedes Danielis palace, Żejtun.

These houses usually have a courtyard leading into a small garden which is divided into two parts by a path.The path was usually covered by a trellis known as '*kanazzata*' for a grape vine, which formed a canopy. The back of the garden was often decorated with a sacred or a female sculpture.

Some houses are larger than others. They have two rooms at the front and another two rooms at the side of the garden. The garden could also include a fountain. The upper floor might have three or four rooms. In such houses there would be enough space for a study room, a music room with a piano, a large kitchen and some rooms for the family's servants. These types of houses are like small palaces (*palazzini*), as their rooms are very spacious and can accomodate a large chest of drawers and other solid mahogany furniture.

All surviving baroque houses are cool in summer and warm in winter. One can admire these houses during Christmas time, when the owners leave windows and main doors open to passers-by to admire the crib, the figure of Baby Jesus and the Christmas tree on display. The latter was introduced after the Second World War. These houses will again be decorated for the parish feast. This time, the balcony will be lit by electric bulbs and a streamer of lights hung on the house's flag pole. All the family's treasures will be on display. These houses will look like little royal residences. Traditionally, these treasures demonstrated the love and respect the breadwinner had towards his family. It also reflected his ability in managing his earned cash as well as the care his wife had towards the belongings of the family.

The Maltese Headgear ('*L-Għonnella*', '*Il-Faldetta*' or '*L-Istamina*')

A well-known characteristic of Maltese folk heritage is the female headgear which is known locally as *'l-għonnella', 'il-faldetta',* or *'l-istamina'*. Many folklore writers consider this headgear to be the Maltese national costume. The *għonnella* can be described as a large hood made of rich silk stiffened at the top by means of cardboard. A part of the *għonnella* rests over the head while it was held by the hands at the sides.

The *għonnella* used to be made in different colours. In the countryside it was either white or green. Sometimes a bride wore a white *għonnella* as headgear for the wedding ceremony. The towns of Żabbar and Żejtun had their own special colour – spotted blue. In the cities, especially in Valletta and Floriana, as well as the Cottonera area – Birgu, Isla and Bormla – the most popular colour for this headgear was black. This colour remained the most popular with Maltese women all over the islands when the *għonnella* was being phased out.

The *għonnella* is still popular among tourists. In souvenir shops one often finds a doll wearing the *għonnella*. These dolls which come in various sizes all wear the black *għonnella*. The *għonnella* was also featured in paintings by the French painter Antoine de Favray. Introduced to Malta by the Knights, he managed to produce a great deal of paintings for the Maltese upper classes. Some of these paintings depict women wearing the lace veils or the *għonnella*. The *għonnella* is still popular in today's art scene, as a recent sculpture placed next to the entrance of the national hospital, Mater Dei, depicts Our Lady with the child Jesus wearing the *għonnella*. Moreover, the *għonnella* used to be a popular feature in former travellers' accounts and other published manuscripts.

It is a popular belief that the *għonnella* appeared in the brief historical period of the French rule. It is said that the *għonnella*

A woman wearing the Maltese female headgear or *għonnella*. Painting by Edward Caruana Dingli.

started to be worn by Maltese women as a protection against the excessive gallantry of the French troops. However, Sir Harry Luke, who was a former Lieutenant-Governor of Malta between the years 1930 and 1938, was of the opinion that the *għonnella* had much older origin. Moreover, it is known that from the 16th to the 18th century, the *għonnella* was worn by women coming from all social classes. This is because these were mentioned in marriage contracts and formed part of the dowry.

Other scholars believe that the *għonnella* developed from a large skirt which was thrown up over the head. It was a common practice in the countries surrounding the Mediterranean Sea for women to put the back part of the upper skirt over their heads. This was still the practice in the countryside after the Second World War. In Turkey, this is called the *'charshaf'*. This tradition developed into a *ċulqana*, which was made of blue cotton with white spots or a flowery design. The *ċulqana* remained in use in the two large communities of the town of Żabbar and its neighbouring town Żejtun. The Żabbar women used to visit several villages and towns wearing this *għonnella* in order to sell capers. These were placed in a cane basket which they had to carry by hand.

Some women had one or two *għonnelli*; but there were others who were luckier, as they had even five. Up to the First World War, the *għonnella* was in general use, but between the wars, it began to fall out of favour.

Some female members of the MUSEUM, a lay religious organisation continued to wear the *għonnella* until quite recently. There were a few women who continued to wear the *għonnella* in the villages especially in Gozo. According to the local newspaper, *The Times* (6 Apr. 1991), the *għonnella* disappeared from the streets of Victoria, Gozo, with the passing away of Ċensa Vella who died at the end of March 1991. She was one of the last Gozitans who was seen wearing the *għonnella* in public. Ċensa Vella was popular with tourists as she was constantly being photographed wearing this headgear. Her memory was kept alive, however, as she was chosen to represent a Maltese woman by the Italian painter Giovanni Battista Conti, who was painting part of the ceiling of the St Lazarus chapel in St George's Basilica in Victoria. The *għonnella* is still used in occasional folk-dancing events and international beauty contests.

There was a time when a new type of *għonnella* was being worn. The original *għonnella* was curtailed for practical purposes and it became known as '*nofs għonnella*' ('half *għonnella*'). However, this never became popular and died a natural death.

The *għonnella* had its share of disadvantages. In church, women used to cover all the view of the main altar when they stood next to each other. Moreover, when two or more women met the it made it difficult to identify them as they obstructed the view of their faces. Finally, in a strong wind, the poor women had to struggle to walk and hold tightly to the *għonnella* in order not to have it blown off.

The octagonal Torri tal-Kaptan in Qrendi. A late medieval fortified tower with 'drop boxes' converted into an elegant residence.

Transport

The Maltese Harbour Boat (*Id-Dgħajsa tal-Pass*)

Malta has a rich patrimony of boats (*dgħajjes*). Unfortunately, some of these boats, such as the Gozitan boat (*id-dgħajsa tal-Latini*), have been lost. Still, we can enjoy a variety of locally made boats which are quite unique. Some popular boats are the *kajjik, luzzu* and *fregatina*. The most popular boat (*dgħajsa*) is the *dgħajsa tal-pass* (the Maltese harbour boat). This boat is

Left: Detail of a Dodge T-110 bus in front of the Tritons fountain, Valletta.

Below: Old postcard showing Maltese *dgħajsas* at Kalkara.

made of a variety of woods, such as mahogany, ash, teak and redwood.

The Maltese harbour boat is mainly seen in the waters of Malta's Grand Harbour (*Il-Port il-Kbi*r). It is a long but elegant boat, which can be quickly rowed across the waters because of its weight. It is used mainly as a passenger boat. Some writers refer to the *dgħajsa tal-pass* as the 'scousin' of the Venetian gondola. However, Joseph Abela, a scholar of local seacrafts, says that this boat's origin is lost in time. He is of the opinion that the *dgħajsa tal-pass* and the gondola are two different boats, as the environmental conditions in which they operate are completely different. He continues to argue that the *dgħajsa tal-pass* has a symmetrical hull while that of the gondola is asymmetrical. Moreover, only the *dgħajsa tal-pass* has a keel.

The earliest pictorial evidence of a *dgħajsa tal-pass* goes back to a work of art created by W. Schellink. This was made during

An old postcard showing a harbour boat approaching Barriera Wharf, Valletta.

his visit to the Islands in 1664. Schellink's work shows a double-ended seafaring craft with washboards (*falki*). These boards are seen alongside the passenger area to protect the passengers against sea spray. Moreover, Shellink's work depicts a boat with short stems which are not perpendicular to the keel. This gives the boat a different profile from the one we see today. Finally, this older version had rowing positions fixed to the front of the boat so that the oarsmen had to look forward while handling the oars. By time, changes were introduced, the most important of which was the increase in length of the two opposing stems. These were meant to help the boatman (*barklor*) to manage his boat better while mooring alongside quays or ship accommodation ladders.

There is a code of practice for managing passengers alighting the *dgħajsa tal-pass*. The boatman is the first to go ashore to prepare for the passengers' disembarkation. Once on dry land, he grabs the fore stem to better control his boat, thus making disembarkation more secure. At the same time, he stretches out his other hand to receive his fees and possibly some tips, while giving advice to passengers about how to leave the boat safely. This advice would include leaving the boat by passing over the triangular monkey deck (*tamburett*) and leaving the boat in alternate sequence to avoid capsizing.

The Maltese harbour boat has its particular characteristics. It should be about 21 feet long, which is the standard length. These boats are painted in the traditional bright maritime colours: red, green and blue. Yellow and white could also be used. The colours are painted in stripes parallel to the waterline or to the curve of the upper border. Some of the boat owners paint their boats in two colours only. This is a tradition which goes back to the times when the British Royal Navy controlled Malta's Grand Harbour. The *barklori*, who had a great admiration for and affection towards the Royal Navy personnel, started painting their boats in the same colour

Dgħajjes tal-pass used to gather around warships to ferry the sailors ashore.

scheme as that employed by this naval power, using only two colours. Each boat has a registration number, which is painted on the upper part of the stems.

Another characteristic is the talisman in the shape of an eye. This is usually painted on the side of the bow. The boatsmen believe that due to the peril and hardships which they have to face on the waters, they need this eye of Osiris to bring good luck. Some other boat owners regard this as the eye of God.

Occasionally, boat owners also included paintings of seagulls, fish or a comet. Moreover, according to Ġuze Cassar Pullicino, a crucifix was placed in a corner inside the boat. Sometimes, next to the crucifix, the *barklori* also placed some dry blessed olive branches they would have obtained from their parish churches after the blessing ceremony of palm and olive leaves held on Palm Sunday.

The *dgħajsa tal-pass* has a long history to narrate. Although the British warships had their own boats, they preferred to ask for the services of the Maltese *barklori*. Many *dgħajjes tal-pass* used to gather around warships to ferry the sailors ashore. By time, the harbour boat became a symbol of the presence of the Royal Navy in Malta. When the last British Naval Commander was about to retire, the residents of Kalkara, the village next to Birgu, presented him with a silver model of the *dgħajsa tal-pass*.

Apart from ferrying sailors ashore, the harbour boat used to be loaded with lace, clothing materials, stationery, souvenirs, sweets, tobacco, coffee, as well as Ceylon tea and other products which were sold to the naval personnel. These products were displayed in boxes, built for the purpose, that were fixed to the boat's sides.

According to Charles Flores, the affection of the Royal Navy towards these harbour boats was shown when a boat was taken by the Royal Navy to Venice to take part in a British Empire-based traditional boat race. The Maltese harbour boat crew were Maltese rowers, who worked at HMS *St Angelo* (the then headquarters of the British power in Malta). The Maltese carried the colours of the day to the delight of those sailors who had gambled a week's beer on it.

The ability of the *barklori* is shown in the two regattas which are held annually inside the Grand Harbour. These regattas take place on 31 March, Malta's Freedom Day, and the feast of the Nativity of Our Lady, known locally as '*il-Bambina*' ('the infant Virgin') or '*il-Victorja*' ('Our Lady of Victories'), which takes place on 8 September. The localities around the Grand Harbour – those of Vittoriosa (Birgu), Cospicua (Bormla), Senglea (l-Isla), Kalkara, Marsa and Marsamxett (the Marsamxett side of Valletta) – take part in all the categories of this race. Birżebbuġa also takes part in these races. They all compete for the Aggregate Shield. The 8 September regatta commemorates the Great Siege victory of the Maltese and the Knights over the Ottoman Turks. At first, according to Charles Flores, it consisted of some Knights' galleys symbolically

Rowers training for the 8 September regatta in the waters of the Grand Harbour.

chasing away the Order's foes from the Grand Harbour. By time, these galleys were replaced by the powerful harbour boats and a regatta was born.

Nowadays, one can see these harbour boats mainly inside the main inlets of the Grand Harbour. They are also found as replicas in maritime museums. Some souvenir shops sell little dainty models and there was a time when small gold or silver brooches were also produced by local gold- and silversmiths. These brooches were especially popular with the female family members of the *barklori*.

Unfortunately, most of the present fleet of harbour boats are over 50 years old. During the days when the British Mediterranean fleet made good use of the harbour, one could find some 200 to 300 boats on the Grand Harbour's waters. However, at one point, quays were built along the Valletta side for the British warships. This was a great blow to the boatsmen as they started losing clients. Today, there are only about 35 harbour boats.

The old harbour boat builders were located mainly at the fishing village of Kalkara. Nowadays, these tradesmen have been replaced by yacht builders and boat repairers. New harbour boats are occasionally commissioned by the regatta clubs. These boats are only taken out for training sessions during the months before the regattas and then they are cleaned and stored for the long winter months, awaiting the next training season to start.

Some *dgħajjes tal-pass* are still being used to ferry people across the Grand Harbour between Birgu and Valletta. This ferry service is run by Mr Whibley. One of his boats is the same one used by Queen Elizabeth II during her stay on the Islands as a naval wife. Between 1949 and 1951, the then Princess Elizabeth would board this red *dgħajsa tal-pass* at Custom House in Valletta to be ferried to HMS *St Angelo* (Fort St Angelo) where her husband, Prince Philip, was stationed. On 21 September 2014, during her grandson's visit to Malta to

A present day boat builder in an old Birgu warehouse.

mark the Islands' 50th anniversary of Independence, the same boat carried Prince William from Birgu to Valletta.

When the Princess used this red boat, it was owned by Carmelo Camilleri. His wife Carmela, was reported by *The Sunday Times of Malta* of 7 September 2014 as saying: 'My husband was proud to ferry her (Princess Elizabeth) – although for him, it was business as usual. She would often stop by and talk to us Maltese – although we didn't understand much English at the time'. The boat spent time stored in an old garage. By time it was in dire need of repair. The boat's renaissance started when Mr Whibley purchased it for the sum of €4,660. It was restored to its former glory to be used as one of the boats for his Valletta–Birgu water taxi business.

The Maltese harbour boat has always been popular with painters, especially maritime ones, such as Giovanni Bonello and the Schranz and Galea dynasties of artists. Their works would end up in the homes of the Royal Navy personnel. Often, these would have been bought from shops located in South Street, Valletta, which specialised in Maltese maritime scenes. Nowadays, these works of art are considered to be auction pieces, and art and history lovers vie with each other to obtain them for their collections.

The Maltese Fishing Boat (*Il-Luzzu*)

Besides the *dgħajsa tal-pass,* Malta can boast of another traditional boat – the Maltese fishing boat known locally as '*il-luzzu*'. The *luzzu*'s origin is lost within the pages of the history books. The first source of light is derived from the 17th-century paintings depicting boats of a design and style very similar to the modern *luzzu*. In former days, the *luzzu* used to have a sail for power. Nowadays, this has been replaced by diesel engines.

A fisherman steering his *luzzu* out of Marsaxlokk harbour.

The building of a *luzzu* is a trade passed on from father to son. The most popular localities where the *luzzijiet* (plural of *luzzu*) are manufactured are Senglea and Kalkara. Both of these lie within the Grand Harbour. The first thing the boat maker does is to prepare the main beam which runs all along the length of the boat. This is called '*il-prim*'. Against this beam smaller supports, referred to as '*il-majjieri*', are fixed. Both the *prim* and the *majjieri* form together the skeleton of the boat.

The next step involves the covering of the skeleton with planks to form the body of the boat. These planks are made from red deal wood. The boat maker examines these planks, one by one, to see if there are any cracks in between. If he finds any, he has to fill them and repaint the whole area where these cracks were found. The whole boat will be painted according to the colours ordered by the fisherman. While painting is taking place, the fisherman hands in the name of the boat to be included in the boat's decorations.

When these boats are not out at sea, they are kept in a special fishing harbour called '*menqa*'. This harbour is rectangular in shape, with a surrounding pavement so that the fishermen can place their fishing nets close to the boats, ready to be taken aboard when needed. There are few examples of a *menqa*. St Paul's Bay has a well-preserved *menqa* in the village core. This harbour is very close to the fishing quarters of this locality. Another *menqa* is found in the main tourist resort of Gozo, Marsalforn. This is located at one end of the bay, very close to the sandy beach. The *menqa* offers a spectacular view of the boats. Some float on the waters of the *menqa* while others lie face down on the pavement for maintenance works.

Apart from the *menqa*, boats are kept in special sheltered inlet harbours. One of these is Wied iż-Żurrieq. This is a natural, narrow inlet, which offers protection from winter storms. Close by there are the small one- or two-roomed stores in which fishermen mend and keep nets. However, when the

Marsaxlokk's open air market is a great place to buy fresh fish.

nets are big, the fishermen mend them in the open. When filled with boats this inlet also offers a wonderful spectacle of colours and crafts.

Another place to see such boats is the fishing village of Marsaxlokk. This area also offers a variety of shops selling fresh fish, as well as fish restaurants all along the bay. These restaurants are usually named after Maltese fish names. Marsaxlokk is one of the best places to see fishermen repairing or preparing their nets and boats to go out to sea. To add to this Mediterranean spectacle, on Sundays, an open air market is organised all along the bay where one can also buy fish and other items. Next to this bay is Malta's experimental centre for the cultivation of fish. Here, fish are bred to supply the many fish farms anchored all around the Islands. This centre is located in one of Alof de Wignacourt's coastal towers.

Another fishing centre in Gozo is Xlendi Bay. Located at the end of a valley, this bay is narrow and is surrounded by high land. This makes it ideal for the sheltering of boats, especially during a winter storm. Next to the pier, there are many restaurants that prepare tasty fish dishes, some of which are typically Maltese. On the pier side of the bay is an open space in which boats are kept for maintenance. Here we also find a stone statue of St Andrew, the patron saint of fishermen. As Xlendi offers a great deal of beautiful scenery, there are also some small hotels, as well as a couple of shops selling locally made objects. A walk along the promenade is a must.

Another Gozo locality associated with fishing is the port of Mġarr. In former days there used to be many more fishing boats here, on both land and water. Nowadays, this man-made port's activity is more commercial. The Gozo ferry operate its boats from here, and on one side,a small marina for boats and yachts has been developed.

The *luzzijiet* need constant maintenance. Their engines, engine compartments and steering equipment need ongoing

Luzzu undergoing maintenance in Marsaxlokk.

checking and servicing. Moreover, the electronic equipment needs to be removed from its place to be checked.

But the most important part of the maintenance work is the checking of the boat's hull. If the bottom of the hull has barnacles and other vegetation that clings to the boat, they have to be removed as they cause the boat to lose speed. To do this, the fisherman or the boat attendant has to use sandpaper to clean the hull and then follow this up by applying a coat of anti-fouling paint. Within a few days the boat is fit again to hit the waters of the *menqa* or other sheltered harbour.

Every five years, the fishermen take their boats for a more thorough check-up. They usually entrust their boats to people who are experts in this type of work. Old paint is completely stripped off so that a close inspection of the craft can be made. Sometimes, the men at work find old planks which need replacing. Other times, the joints between the planks need to be opened and resealed. The tradesman who carries out this delicate work is called *'il-qalfat'*. It is he who checks every single joint. It is worthwhile mentioning that a *luzzu* has hundreds of joints all over its body. For small joints, the *qalfat* uses putty, while for the major joints he stuffs the gaps with a thick gauze-like material called *'ix-xoqqa'*, which is covered in liquid tar. This is left to dry up and solidify, after which putty is applied. The final work consists of sanding the putty. This usually takes place after a few days. The *luzzu* is then repainted in the family's traditional colours.

When maintenance work is ready, the fisherman loses no time to take his boat to sea. In fine weather he leaves the *menqa* with his boat and nets and heads out to his favourite fishing grounds. Sometimes, he spends days away at sea. On his return he has to see how to sell his catch. There are two selling methods. A member of the family, usually his wife, does the round of different towns or villages to sell the fish.

A Maltese *luzzu* sits in the waters of Pietà creek.

The other option is to sell through the fish 'depot'. Here, fish are grouped together and placed in plastic containers. They are then sold as a bundle by means of bidding. The highest bidder gets the whole container. Usually, the buyers are people who run restaurants or hotels. Some of the fish are also sold to fish shops, which, at present, have increased in number.

The fisherman needs to protect his *luzzu*. He has to take note of the weather. In autumn and winter the fisherman does his best to avoid storms as he knows quite well that a violent storm could easily reduce his craft to bits and pieces. It is rather sad to see *luzzijiet* after a storm: half-sunk, capsized or wrecked. It is no wonder that a fisherman starts thinking about sheltering his boat around the beginning of December. Summer is the best season for fishermen. This season brings along the cash fish of the year: *lampuki* (dolphin fish). Fishing for *lampuki* starts around 15 August. It will continue until November or the early days of December. The Maltese housewife knows quite well

Lampuki and octopus are both favourites with local housewives.

The eye of Osiris is meant to ward off the evil eye.

how to prepare special dishes which include *lampuki*. The most popular are the *lampuki* pie and fried *lampuki*, served with potatoes and vegetables.

The *luzzu* has its own culture. Each fisherman has his family's heritage of colours, which are passed on from father to son. Even to this day, we find fishermen still using the colours that belonged to their grandfathers. These are very rarely changed. They believe that a colour change would bring bad luck. The old fishermen were very superstitious. They believed in the evil eye, so made sure that the eye of Osiris decorated the body of their boat.

The Marsaxlokk fishermen like to invite the parish priest to bless the boats and nets at the start of the *lampuki* season. This ceremony takes place around 15 August. All the fishermen try to get a small piece of dry olive branch, which is blessed on Palm Sunday, to be placed next to a crucifix fixed underneath the main shelf of the boat.

The Malta Bus (*Il-Karozza tal-Linja*)

The first mechanised land public transport in Malta was the train. This was inaugurated in 1883 and had only one line, the Valletta–Mtarfa line. The railway passed through Floriana, Ħamrun, Santa Venera, Birkirkara, Attard, Rabat, Mdina and Mtarfa. It was created mainly to serve the people employed with the British Services, to reach home as quickly as possible. The Maltese could use this means of transport, but tickets were rather expensive. In 1905 two new types of transport were introduced. These were the tram and the buses.

At first, privately-owned buses were used. These buses were introduced by an Englishman who brought some vehicles over to Malta to start transporting people to and from the most popular spots of the island. The first team of buses consisted of a single-decker, four double-deckers and a lorry. They were introduced at a time when many Maltese were trying to find

2851, 'Lusitania' named after the *Cunard* liner torpedoed on 7 May, 1915.

Number 1784 - Ford, Sliema route.

the ideal means of transport. There were many problems to solve, such as narrow and steep streets. The first buses were known as 'matchboxes'. These started functioning with a very limited timetable.

The tram served some areas of Malta which the train did not cover, mainly Raħal Ġdid (Paola). The Grand Harbour cities were joined by ferry boats owned by the Senglea Mattei family. The horse-drawn big cab, known as the 'omnibus', was stationed at Lija and used to operate from this locality to Valletta. Small horse-driven cabs operated from all parts of Malta with the exemption of streets with steep slopes.

At first, buses faced all this competition, but as they were tailored-made for Malta, they became the most popular means of public transport. In 1922, the first scheduled bus service started to operate. This was run by the British Motor Company (BMC) which had been set up by the German brothers two years before. By that same year, there were about 50 buses which were built locally with either a Ford or a Chevrolet

Number 1390, Cospicua.

chassis. These buses, about 16 in all, had a balcony-shaped opening on the rear of the bus. Because of this, they became popularly known as '*tal-gallarija*' ('of the balcony').

In 1926, the number of licensed buses reached 108. Well-to-do families started to invest in this means of transport. They would buy a bus engine and then order the bus body from a local carpenter who built wooden bus frames. One person who invested in buses for the Sliema and St Julian's route was Dr Joseph Gasan. By time, Dr Gasan switched to another type of business, when he founded a company which sold private cars. During the 1930s, two major companies started operating on the Sliema routes. These were the BMC and the Sliema Bus Company. Before the Second World War, more elegant and stylised vehicles appeared on the Maltese roads. These new buses had a passenger access door at the back. This door was later removed and placed in a more convenient location, close to the front of the bus.

During the 1960s, a new design appeared in Malta buses. These buses were referred to as having 'Front Control'. One bus was a special one. It was operated by Gasan under licence from the Posts Department to carry Gozitan mail. This bus was painted grey with a red cheatline. It used to be parked by the building of then General Post Office in Merchants Street, Valletta. Passengers who wished to go to Gozo could use this bus to take them to Marfa, where the Gozo ferryboat used to berth. This service stopped when the Mellieħa buses took over. Moreover, there were also 'private' buses painted light yellow and their job was to transport people to places of work or entertainment.

As the service was extended to cover the entire island of Malta, buses of the same route were painted in the same colour. Examples of these were the Mellieħa buses, which were painted bluish white with a dark blue cheatline; the Birkirkara and Ħamrun buses, which were all red; and the Sliema and St

Number 2272, Birkirkara–Ħamrun.

Julian's buses, which were a dark green colour with a darker green cheatline.

All these buses operated from Valletta. This locality had two termini. One was at *Porta Reale* or Kingsgate (also called '*Bieb il-Belt*' or City Gate), the former entrance to Valletta, while the other was at Castile Place, in front of the then British Services main office, Auberge de Castile.

By time, the local government wanted all privately-owned buses to become part of one company and all the different colours had to disappear. They were painted in light green, the colour used by the buses of the Cottonera cities. Then, after a second bus reform, the colour was again changed to bus colours formerly used by the Żebbuġ line, that is, bright yellow with an orange cheatline.

As the buses were privately-owned they were decorated as if they were an extension of private homes. This imprint was

The bus terminus just outside Valletta in the early 1960s.

Niche inside a Maltes bus with a figure of the Pietà Madonna and Christ.

important to the bus owners, who wanted to tell everybody that the buses they were driving were theirs. Some decorated the driver's window with a pair of curtains. In the space above this internal window there would often be a niche with an image of the owner's patron saint, or that of Our Lady or Jesus Christ. Next to this niche came the name of the bus, such as 'Queen Mary', 'Ben Hur', 'Tom Mix', among others, as well as the number of seated passengers the bus could carry and the bus registration number. At the door was a sort of bin where the passengers could dispose of their used tickets. Sometimes, the dashboard and windscreen were also decorated either with football stickers or flags. Some drivers placed family photographs there too.

At first, each bus offered employment for two people: the driver, who was most probably the owner of the bus or a member of his family, and a young boy, who would probably have just left school, to act as a bus conductor. The people

This Fordson Thames ET7 has been retained for nostalgic tours.

used to wait for their bus at different stages marked by a dark blue sign bearing the words 'Bus Stop'. Stages where the fare changed were marked by red signs bearing the words 'Fare Stage'.

The buses followed a particular route according to a set timetable. Sometimes, when the bus was off duty, the owner could hire his bus for a private function. Such functions included visits to major shrines organised by parish priests or outings to a beach organised by local band clubs for their supporters on the day following the village feast. On the latter occasion, people would spend a day swimming, singing and eating. Until the days after the Second World War, people used to carry heavy baskets full of food and drink, and inside each bus there would be musicians with musical instruments who would play all the way to and from the beach. Sometimes a folk singer would also accompany the music players. Nowadays, these Maltese buses are a relic of the past. They have become a tourist attraction.

Finally, a traditional Maltese bus has been turned into a souvenir shop in Malta, while in Adelaide, Australia, a Maltese–Australian, Tanya Agius, and her father bought another traditional Maltese bus and transformed it into a *pastizzi* kiosk.

The Horse-drawn Cab (*Il-Karrozzin*)

On your visit to Valletta, the capital of Malta or Mdina, the former capital city, you might see a horse-drawn cab passing by, which the Maltese refer to as '*il-karrozzin*'. This was a means of transport that was very popular with the Maltese during the 19th and early 20th centuries. Some writers believe that it was introduced from the British colony of Gibraltar during the middle of the 19th century.

Il-karrozzin, the Maltese horse-drawn cab.

An old Maltese postcard showing a *karrozzin* in Bastion Street, Mdina.

The secret of the popularity of this means of transport lies in the fact that before it was introduced on the local market, several alterations were made to make it suit the needs of the local scene. The *karrozzin* survived the first test when it had to compete with the 'omnibus', which was a larger cart driven by more horses.

The *karrozzin* offered several advantages to the Maltese, the first being that it was small and so could pass through the streets of Valletta, Mdina, Birgu and the villages, all of which are quite narrow. It could also be used for short distances. Thus, one could load the *karrozzin* with merchandise to be transported to another nearby locality. The *karrozzin* operated without a set timetable and could stop anywhere the passenger desired. This meant that the passengers could negotiate the journey and time with the owner of the *karrozzin*. This horse-drawn cart offered a safe and comfortable journey. Its tent offered a further comfort as passengers could be protected from the direct rays of the sun, rain or wind. Finally, it offered privacy. The *karrozzin* could only carry up to a maximum of four persons. If there was a fifth person, they would have to sit next to the *karrozzin* driver (*il-kuċċier*). This meant that a private conversation could take place as the two *karrozzin* seats faced each other. The tent curtains could also be drawn to offer more privacy to the passengers.

In former days, one could board a *karrozzin* from St Lucia Street in Valletta. It was here that many horse-drawn carts met waiting for passengers to show up. This was an ideal place for a terminus being next to Valletta's major street, Kingsway (now known as Republic Street). The *karrozzin* terminus was later transferred to Palace Square. It is now found next to the cruise liners terminus, on the Valletta side of the Grand Harbour. From the towns and villages one had to contact an owner of a *karrozzin* personally and negotiate a time when the driver could be waiting for his passengers to start the planned journey.

The *karrozzin* was seldom used by the village people. When they had to travel between villages, they usually went on foot. If they had to transport bulky objects they usually called a farmer to help them with his farm cart. This cart could carry a larger load for a short distance. However, the *karrozzin* was used by the village people to share their happy and sad moments. If someone had to appear in court, they had to leave in the early hours of the day by *karrozzin* to Valletta to be able to wait in one of the corridors of the Palace of Justice. The *karrozzin* was also used by young people and their parents to attend a graduation, or by a priest who was asked by the curia authority to report an incident or some other personal communication.

The *karrozzin* was used by the cultural elite to go to the Royal Opera House located at the entrance to the capital city. The ruling elite could enter the theatre's premises through a side door still riding the *karrozzin*. It must have been quite a spectacle to see Malta's elite entering or leaving the theatre. The ladies were dressed up in long garments with feathers in their hair. Around their necks they wore diamonds or Maltese-made gold jewellery. The most popular Maltese gold necklace was known as '*ta' Gran spinat*'. Another type of gold jewellery was made in *filugranu* style: a method of creating gold jewellery without using too much gold. Rings were also popular and a number of these were worn on both hands. All sorts of rings were used but the most popular were the precious stone rings, the most prestigious of which was the ruby ring.

Males were always dressed up in black with a white silk shirt. They wore bow ties and scarves around their necks. In their waistcoats, they would have had a chain (*polka*) tied to a gold clock. Usually, all these precious objects were either given to the couple before marriage as part of the dowry, or would have been bought by the couple after marriage.

The *karrozzin* is made up of a cart with two seats each of which can accommodate two adults. The cart is built on four wheels, two small ones at the front and two larger ones at the back. The two seats are covered by a tent which has four pairs of curtains. These curtains are usually tied up and the passenger could untie them according to his or her wishes. The driver sits on a two seater in front of the passengers' seats. His seat is not sheltered from the rays of the sun, wind or rain. Next to the driver's seat is a small lantern which is lit during the night and a bell which serves as a horn. The *karrozzin* is always driven by one horse.

The driver has a special love towards his horse. He takes care of this animal day by day offering him the best barley on the market and providing him with an adequate amount of water to drink. In the past, there used to be water stations offering fresh water for the horses. Two such water stations still exit: one is near Argotti Gardens in Floriana and the second used to be located at the entrance of Republic Street. The latter was re-located several times and is considered to be a relic of the past.

Riding in a *karrozzin* is an unusual experience. One can watch the traffic and the people going by. The best *karrozzin* experience is offered at Mdina, where the streets are narrow and long. When the *karrozzin* passes by, the sounds of the cart wheels and those of the horse's hoofs on the granite street stones are something the passenger will not forget for many days. The Maltese have forgotten about the service of the *karrozzin*. It is too slow for their present day use. Only some young and old people who have never experienced a *karrozzin* ride opt for such a means of transport. The tourists also enjoy a ride, especially through the streets of Valletta or Mdina, both during day-time and at night.

A horse-drawn *karrozzin* waits for fares in Bastion Square, Mdina.

Entertainment

Carnival (*Il-Karnival*)

At present, there are two types of Carnival festivities being held annually in Malta. The traditional Carnival is held during the week before the start of Lent (Ash Wednesday). This Carnival has a long history as well as traditions and typical sweets associated with it. It is held mainly at Valletta and Floriana, as well as Victoria, Gozo. Moreover, other localities organise their own typical Carnival festivities, known as mini-Carnivals. Another Carnival is held in summer. This was introduced in 2008 thanks to the initiative of the St Paul's Bay Local Council, and entrusted its organisation to Mr Paul Chetcuti.

The traditional Carnival starts on the last Thursday before Lent. On this day, a ceremony is held in Valletta, where the Carnival flag is raised and the Carnival anthem is played. This is followed by the Carnival traditional dance, popularly known as '*il-Parata*' together with some other dancing. On the following day, Carnival activities are held at the Carnival enclosure, where the Carnival anthem is once again played followed by dancing competitions. Finally, a défilé is organised throughout the main streets and squares of Valletta, headed by a special float – the King Carnival float. In this défilé, all the decorated

Carnival scene in St George's Square, Valletta *c.*1900.

triumphal floats, floats with people dressed in costumes, carts and cabs, together with bands of bandmasters in grotesque attire playing lively marches, take part. Sometimes, men dress up as women, and vice-versa, the women in men's clothes.

On Saturday, the Children's Carnival is held. In the morning, the celebration starts with the playing of the Carnival anthem, followed by dancing inside the enclosure. Finally, the King Carnival float enters the enclosure and another défilé is organised. In the afternoon, the Carnival anthem is played once again followed by competitive dancing. The Grand Défilé then makes its way through the main Valletta streets and squares. At night, a general merrymaking activity takes place with the participation of live bands and dancing, where the public is invited to take part.

On Sunday another Grand Défilé is organised, this time starting from Castile Place in Valletta and ending in the

Children and adults alike flock to Valletta during Carnival weekend to see the brightly coloured triumphal floats.

enclosure. More dancing competitions for adults are held on Monday morning followed by another Grand Défilé also in Valletta. On the last day of Carnival, general merrymaking is held in the morning along Republic Street with the participation of bands, grotesque masks and dance companies. The Grand Finale takes place on Floriana's main street – St Anne's. This défilé includes floats, dance companies in costumes, grotesque masks and bands. A fireworks display ends the Carnival festivities.

Gozo organises its own Carnival centred at Independence Square, Victoria (known as '*It-Tokk*'). As in Malta, Carnival here is celebrated throughout the five days preceding Ash Wednesday. On Saturday, the children's Carnival is held in the morning while on Sunday, a general défilé is held along the main streets of Victoria in the afternoon. This is followed by a special entertainment programme at the same square where dancers in costumes and floats take part.

Carnival is not only centred in the main cities of Malta and Gozo. Some localities organise their own typical Carnival. Nadur in Gozo holds two types of Carnival. An organised Carnival is held in this locality consisting of a variety of bands, floats, dances, costumes and the traditional cockaigne ('*Kukkanja*'). However, the main attraction of the Nadur Carnival is the spontaneous one held during the night. One can see people dressed in masks walking up and down from the main square through one of the side streets. People wear all sorts of funny and grotesque costumes, some carrying placards daubed with remarks insulting public or private personalities. Some costumes are satirical. The Nadur floats are little more than carts, but they also carry a message besides adding to the general merrymaking atmosphere.

Xagħra, another Gozitan locality, also has its own Carnival. In the main village square, a varied Carnival festivity takes place, where one can see dances and other Carnival

Nadur carnival in Gozo rivals Valletta's in popularity but surpasses it in spontaneity and revelry.

competitions such as the cockaigne. But the main attraction of this Carnival is the *Kummittiva* dances. Here, a typical dance company, whose members inherit the right to take part, have a whole repertoire of several types of dances. Two other Gozitan villages that organise Carnival activities are Xewkija and Għarb. Xewkija organises a Carnival défilé consisting of floats with the participation of its local band, the Prekursur Band.

Għarb has another spontaneous Carnival. Here, dancing, singing, as well as a costume competition, take place. Back to Malta, in Qormi, we find Carnival band marches with bandmasters from the three Qormi band clubs all dressed up in costumes. There is also the participation of various dance companies and grotesque masks. The Mellieħa Carnival consists mainly of band marches by one of its bands, the Società Filarmonika La Vittoria. St Julian's and Għaxaq also have their own Carnival activities. The Għaxaq Carnival is similar to that of Nadur and is held along one of the parish church side streets and in the main square.

Tarxien used to organise a typical spontaneous Carnival. Young men wrapped up in with white bed sheets, a broom and a candle lantern used to turn up in front of the village's cemetery before sunset. They used to cut two small holes in these sheets to be able to see while walking along the streets hidden under these sheets. Before starting, they used to decide the route, usually including the houses where their sweethearts or favourite girls lived. They used to walk with the lit lantern in one hand and the broom in the other. When they arrived in front of the house of their loved ones, they would bang the broom against the wooden balcony to create a haunting sound, disturbing the whole family, especially the parents of the young girls. Sometimes, when the parents had had enough of the banging, they would prepare a bucket of cold water to throw over the young men. This traditional Tarxien custom was referred to as the 'Ghost Carnival' ('*Tal-Erwieħ*').

Recently a special Carnival started to be organised for persons with intellectual disabilities. This includes band playing, costume parades, mini floats, collages and mask exhibitions, as well as dancing. Since 2014, they also started to take part in the Valletta Carnival.

Carnival in Malta has a long history; its origins trace back to the early 1400s. It has been recorded that at the general hospital in Rabat, patients were given special meals for this festivity. Carnival festivities increased during the times of the Order. The traditional *Parata* – the sword-dance marking the victory of the Maltese and the Knights against the Turks in 1565 – was introduced. This dance was given great importance during the rule of the Order. One of the Order's officials used to visit the Grand Master to remind him to issue the permission to allow the Maltese to dance in the *Parata*. Then, a stone tied to a rope was hung against the balcony of the Castellania, Valletta's law court. This meant that for the next three days laws were not enforced. A popular saying among the Maltese peasants said: 'No *Parata* no Carnival'. When the permission was granted, the *Parata* was danced in Valletta's main square, St George's Square, also known as Palace Square. When the dancers left, they would continue with their performances in front of wealthy families' residences so that they could earn a few coins.

The *kukkanja* or *coccagna* was also introduced during the Order's rule. A tall trunk of a tree used to be placed against the wall and among its small branches were tied all sorts of food. The general public was allowed to run and climb the trunk to pick items of food and the lucky ones were allowed to take them home. A ball was placed at one point of the *coccagna*. When someone reached this ball it would open and a figure

Mid-nineteenth century *coccagna* held in Palace Square, Valletta.

Typical late eighteenth century Maltese Carnival scene.

would appear. The lucky person would earn a little sum of money given to him by the Grand Master.

Although Carnival was alien to the British, it still continued to flourish with some historical incidents during the British rule. The *Veljuni,* or public masked balls, were held in major theatres in Valletta. The Governor used to organise a masked ball where middle and upper class Maltese used to dress up in costumes to attend. During this ball, *il-Maltija,* an aristorictic dance was danced. Those taking part used to wear 18th-century costumes.

When Malta was granted the 1921 Constitution, things started to change. Carnival was a case in point. Since 1926, the outdoor Carnival festivities in Valletta have been organised by a special committee. Carnival started to include a défilé of floats, carts and cabs featuring imaginative figures full of colour. These floats started to be manned by young people who used to blow their whistles, throw coloured paper confetti, sound horns and bang on the sides of the floats. Industrialists used to sponsor part of the expense of a float. They used to pass advertisement papers to the float personnel to distribute to bystanders.

Up to 1974, a part of Valletta's main square was fenced off in to create an enclosure. This offered space for dancing. In 1974, the enclosure was taken to Freedom Square, but when this was closed for the building of Parliament, the enclosure was taken back to St George's Square.

In pre-war days, many people could be seen masquerading through the streets. Some dressed up as ghosts, demons, dominoes and Pierrots, while some simply wore a mask and walked along the main streets of the locality. During those

Political satire: An early twentieth-century pro-Italian faction carnival float implying that Malta was about to be buried by British Imperialism.

days, it was a customary for people in masks to be sieged by *pastizzi* throwers in Valletta's main street.

In former days, Carnival floats contained some elements of political satire. Grotesque masked men danced their way through the streets and squares of Valletta. At one point, these were banned as sometimes, public figures were offended. In 2014, this tradition was revived and floats and grotesque masks could once more represent members of parliament in a satirical manner.

A characteristic of the Maltese Carnival is the *qarċilla*. This is a comedy acted out in public first in Valletta and then in the villages. A 'notary' reads out a marriage agreement between an engaged couple. The contract is full of jokes and biting satirical comments. According to scholars, this originated around the year 1760 and the first *qarċilla* was written by a member of the clergy, Dun Feliċ Demarco. This custom came to an end about a century ago due to the trouble it caused. However, it was revived in 2014.

Carnival boosts business. Street hawkers and shopkeepers start preparing for these days well ahead. They start selling coloured caps, whistles and trumpets. Children, young men and women buy plastic water pistols to shoot water at each other. This custom is not welcomed by everybody, and some incidents do occur due to these 'pistol battles'.

Confectioneries and sweet shops start selling the traditional pyramid sweet known as the '*prinjolata*'. The Maltese *prinjolata* is similar to its Sicilian 'cousin', with a small difference in shape. Apart from the *prinjolata* there are sugared almonds called '*perlini*'.

In the last day of Carnival there used to be the custom of burning a coffin. This was a symbolic ritual intended to make everyone remember that the merrymaking days were over and Lent would start within a few hours.

Back to the present day, the Malta Summer Carnival takes place in the Buġibba and Qawra coastal areas. About ten floats and several dance companies take part. Activities are usually spread over two days. On Saturday, a défilé is organised from the St Paul's Bay core area to a square in Qawra. The route is mainly along the coastal road. The next day this défilé starts from another Qawra square and it goes through one of Qawra's main streets, which is full of hotels and restaurants. These défilés are followed by dancing in the main Buġibba square.

The Feast (*Il-Festa*)

In every locality, large or small, a feast is organised in honour of either the patron saint (*festa titulari*) or the 'second in importance' saint (*festa sekondarja*). Not all parishes have two annual feasts. Some parishes have only one. In the parishes with two traditional feasts, rivalry between one group of parishioners and the other will be at its best starting from a week or two before the feast day in question. This is manifested through the programme of activities organised by band clubs and confraternities.

Feasts are occasions of great rejoicing. This is further expressed through enriched church decorations, liturgical functions, street illuminations, fireworks, band programmes and open-air entertainment. Some feasts have particular traditions. A case in point is the water regatta held during the feast of Our Lady's Nativity celebrated at l-Isla, a seaside locality.

With only a few exceptions, the majority of localities organise their feasts between April and September. This period of time is referred to by the locals as the '*festa* season'. Only the parishes of St Paul's Shipwreck (one of the three Valletta parishes), St Joseph (Rabat, Malta) and the Immaculate

Conception (Bormla) organise their feasts according to the Church's liturgical calendar.

Feast celebrations fall into two categories: those held inside the church, and those held in the streets, squares and band clubs of the parish. Church feast helpers start planning for some two months beforehand. The first thing the church sexton and his helpers do is to give a good spring cleaning to the church. All walls are cleaned, electric bulbs checked and all maintenance carried out. The walls are then covered with red damask and chandeliers are hung in the arches alongside the aisle. A canopy is placed over the main altar. Before the *Novena* (nine days of religious preparations) starts, the statue is taken out of its niche and placed on a sculptured, box-shaped plinth. It is decorated with a set of six large candlesticks. While the *Novena* is going on, the altars and other religious items inside the church are decorated with precious and artistic objects.

Sunday morning festivities during the feast of Christ the King, Paola.

The *Novena* consists of nine days of special liturgical functions involving sacred music. This ends three days before the feast day. These last days are called three days of '*Tridu*' in which special prayers and singing are held in the church. On the last day of the '*Tridu*', a special procession with the relic of the saint is held from a nearby chapel to the parish church. All the members of the parish clergy and confraternity members – '*fratelli*' – take part in this procession.

On the feast day itself, several masses are said in church. A mass that includes music and a special sermon about the virtues of the saint is said in the morning. In the evening, the most important external event takes place. This is the procession with the saint's statue through the streets and squares of the locality. The rejoicement reaches its peak when the statue is about to re-enter the church. At this point, the square in front

Mosta church lights up for the feast of the Assumption of Our Lady.

of the church is full of people singing, clapping, praying and watching the fireworks display. This popular emotional expression of happiness is call '*briju*'. Some say it is 'in their blood' to celebrate with all this pomp and gaiety.

Outdoor festivities are mainly organised by the supporters of the band clubs. The main streets are decorated with flags, banners, street steamers, paper decorations and electric lights. One can also see wooden pillars on top of which life-sized statues of saints and angels are placed. Usually, the angel figures hold brackets with electric lamps. In the squares, large groups of statues are placed on wooden pillars featuring saints, popes, bishops, doctors of the church, episodes from the life of the saint and personalities of the Old and New Testaments. Some wooden poles are decorated with trophy banners featuring Maltese, the Order's and the Vatican colours. These flag poles originated from the military weapons used during bygone sieges. During the '*tridu*' days, sellers erect their stands displaying white or dark brown nougat (*qubbajt*). Some sell fast food, cool drinks and other delicacies.

The spirit of the feast is enriched with the evening playing of band marches throughout the streets and squares for a whole week before the feast day. People flock to walk behind the bandmasters, dancing and singing along to the playing of marches. Some band clubs organise special concerts in the main square on a grand bandstand (*planċier*). Many localities organise a special band march parade for youths during the early afternoon on the feast day. This parade is very colourful as it includes people dressed up in the band club's colours. Sometimes, the supporters' faces are also painted in the same colours. While the band plays, supporters drink and some strong young men carry their sweethearts on their shoulders and dance to the rythm of the band march. On the feast day, several bands belonging to other localities, are invited to play during the feast evening activities. In some localities it is a

The statue of St Helen is proudly carried through the streets of Birkirkara.

custom to invite a band to play even during the procession. This band usually plays religious and lively band marches.

The feast is a special day for all the family. Before the feast day, the whole family used to leave the locality and head to Valletta to buy new dresses, shoes and handbags. The houses used to be decorated with the latest furnishings and the chandelier covers would be brought down making the house a miniature royal palace. Even the house fronts used to be whitewashed. Nowadays, the wooden and open house balconies are decorated with electric bulbs as well as banners showing a portrait of the saint.

On the feast day, the whole family is united for lunch. Sometimes, guests are also invited to attend this lunch, including any visiting emigrants. Lunch is usually a special one in which all the members sit around a large table decorated with fine cutlery and tableware. A special linen tablecloth, a low lying vase with flowers, and lit candlesticks all form part of the festive scenes. All items are usually used thrice a year – for Christmas, Easter and the feast lunch.

Fireworks are also manufactured by the supporters of the band clubs. On the eve of the feast, the air fireworks starts the show, lighting up the dark sky with many colours and filling the air with noise. Then the ground fireworks are displayed, one by one, an hour before midnight. Many people leave their houses and crowd the square to admire this spectacle. If the square is by the sea, some families take a boat to watch the display while enjoying the sea breeze.

Before returning home, when the feast comes to an end, families usually stop at one of the nougat stands to buy two blocks of nougat, one white and one dark brown. Some also buy some small blocks to offer to friends and workmates when they return to work. The day following the feast day is not a working day for many workers. It has been a custom for whole families and close friends to spend this day on a beach. This is called '*xalata*'.

For the *xalata,* families share cars decorated with paper decorations. Some join buses hired by the band club. In the past, these buses used to host two or three instrument players. On the way to and from the beach, the people would sing loudly accompanied by guitars and accordions. The day on the beach is spent swimming, drinking, eating a packed lunch and enjoying the company of friends and family. When the *xalata* is over, a carcade is formed touring the streets and squares of the locality. This creates a carnivalesque atmosphere.

A week later, the statue is taken from its plinth and placed inside its niche in the church. From that moment on, the parishioners start dreaming, planning and contributing towards the next feast, trying to improve on the previous one.

Fireworks

In Malta, town and village feasts are mainly held throughout the summer months. One of the main characteristics of these folk festivals are the fireworks or civilian pyrotechnics. In Malta, fireworks were first introduced by the Knights who used to hold fireworks displays in honour of St Barbara. The Maltese enjoyed themselves watching these fireworks light up the night sky and with the help of some Sicilians, they quickly learned the skills of firework production.

At first, during a town or village feast, several soldiers employed by the Knights, were asked to gather on the church parvis before the beginning of the feast procession. They were expected to fire a salute in honour of the saint whose feast was being celebrated. This tradition was later replaced by the firing of *maskli* – mug-shaped 'tins', made of iron or bronze, which when filled with powder and set alight, produced a

Ground fireworks (*ġiġġifogu*) consist mainly of Catherine wheels.

Air fireworks light up the skies above the town of Mellieħa.

loud sound. During the 18th century, these *maskli* were in turn replaced by fireworks, which by time became part and parcel of the religious feasts celebrations.

During a feast three types of fireworks are displayed. There is the ground fireworks display (*ġiġġifogu*) which takes place close to midnight on the eve of the feast, consisting mainly of Catherine wheels. There are also light fireworks, which are set off on the roofs of buildings and are referred to as '*musketterija*' or '*trikki-trakki*'. These are mainly used as signals for the start of the main activities such as the band programme or the feast procession. Nowadays, *stoppini* (light coloured bombs), which, when displayed carry a silver or gold 'tail', have started to be used too.

The third type of fireworks are the air fireworks that include several variations such as the *murtali tal-kuluri*. When displayed, these produce flower-shaped images, usually in red, yellow, green, white and blue. However, other colours are also being introduced. Air fireworks are mainly used on the eve of the feast as well as on the feast day. Apart from the *murtali tal-kuluri* there is the *murtalun,* which when displayed produces a very loud noise. In the past, these were used at dawn to remind everyone that the feast was being celebrated on that day. These have now lost their popularity. There is also the traditional *salut* (the salute), consisting of 21 very loud bombs, representing the international salute which an army gives to a head of state and head of government.

The most popular fireworks display is the *kaxxa infernali.* This consists mainly of similar or different types of bombs. The most commonly used are: *tal-bomba* (bomb); *tal-ispanjola* (Spanish); *tas-sfafar* (whistles); *tal-kulur* (coloured); *tal-beraq pront* (quick lightning); *tad-dañna* (smoky); and *murtaletti f'nofshom* (interval light bombs). The size of the *kaxxa infernali* is calculated by the number of bombs displayed in continuous sequence. Two days

The statue of Our Lady of Pompei enters the parish church of Marsaxlokk to the sounds and smells of air fireworks.

As Maltese as it gets - *luzzi* in the water and fireworks in the sky.

after the feast day, the villagers or townsmen boast about the number of bombs the *kaxxa infernali tal-ħruġ* consisted of.

This *kaxxa infernali* is considered to be the main fireworks display carried out according to the village or town's traditions. The traditional air displays are generally held throughout the nine days of the *Novena*: when the statue is taken out of its niche, the start of band marches, the transition (the carrying of the saint's relic from a nearby chapel to the church held on the eve of the feast day), and the start and end of the feast procession. At some points of the feast procession, a special air fireworks display also takes place. A case in point is Żabbar. When the procession of Our Lady of Graces reaches the *Misraħ* area, a special air fireworks display is set off. This is considered by some as the major air display of this locality.

There are other types of bombs used during a feast day. We find the *serpentelli* (serpents) that produce serpentine lights. Others are called *'murtaletti tad-daħna tal-kulur'* ('coloured

The careful orchestration of ground fireworks is impressive.

smoke bombs'). These are mainly used during daylight, especially in the morning during the High Mass (*il-Kantata*). The *tiri tal-wieħed wieħed* are also popular especially during the Gozitan feasts. These bombs are displayed from time to time, one by one and are also referred to as '*tir*' (shot).

Fireworks are produced on a parish level. They are made in the *kamra tan-nar* (fireworks factory) built on the outskirts of the locality. The person in charge of fireworks production is a holder of a police licence. The fireworks factory consists of two sections, a workshop and a store. The running of these fireworks factories are governed by strict rules that every one has to follow. Safety is of utmost importance while working in these factories.

Although there is great danger in fireworks production still the Maltese continue to nurture a special love towards them. The recipes for manufacturing particular bombs are considered to be a closely guarded secret. This is mainly due to the rivalry that exists between the different localities and between the various band clubs found in the parish itself.

The displays are becoming more and more elaborate and spectacular. The most popular are those of Lija and Imqabba.

Traditional Folk Singing (*L-Għana*)

Sometime in their history, Spain, Sicily and Malta have all witnessed North African occupation. This left an imprint on the lifestyles and cultures of their people. A characteristic of this influence is the melody and verse-rendering of folk singing. This imprint is manifested in flamenco singing in Spain, while in Sicily, we can hear it in either the *filastrocca* or *cantastorie*. In Malta, this cultural influence is found in *għana*. This singing has been defined by Charles Coleiro as '...a composition of amoeban jingles improvised on the spur of the moment and answered by an equally extemporised verse.'

Għana is sung by two or more singers called '*għannejja*', who seat themselves at two opposite ends of the stage, retorting answers to each other in rhyme without any planning or meditation. *Għannejja* vie with each other regarding their ability to sing without searching for words. The theme varies according to the circumstances of popular interest. In some instances, satire is also used, dealing with the faults or character of the singers themselves. The singing involves musical accompaniment by three guitarists. The lead guitarist is called '*Il-Prim*' (the prime). Between each stanza of *għana*, the lead guitarist plays *il-prejjem* in which he or she shows their skills at guitar playing.

The tunes are somewhat wild in general, but they also involve romantic beauty and harmony. As the singing starts, the audience tries to follow all the words being sung closely. Clarity of expression in the performance is expected out of every *għannej*. Moreover, the audience also expects singing to include correct rhyming and a theme that is maintained throughout the song.

There are various types of *għana*. The *spirtu pront*, which is the most popular type of, consists of short stanzas, normally sung by a group of two or more singers. This type of folk singing takes place in the form of a song duel. This generally has two styles of singing. The first style is called 'the hitting back'. If four singers are involved, the first singer sings with the third person, while the second singer does his or her part with the fourth singer.

The second style is known as the 'impromptu reply'. While the singer starts his or her first two lines, the second singer continues the rest of the stanza. It is normal practice for the singer who finishes the last two verses to start the next stanza. This is called '*għanja maqsuma*' or '*għana bil-qasma*' which means

The guitar player by local artist Edward Caruana Dingli (1876-1950).

broken or shared singing. Sometimes, this type of singing is also referred to as '*nofs għanja*' meaning half singing. This *spirtu pront* and the *għana bil-qasma* require a great deal of quick thinking as well as the ability to rhyme. Singing usually lasts for an hour and comes to an end with a *kadenza*, which has two or more stanzas.

Another type of *għana* is the *għana tal-fatt*. This consists of a long and elaborate narrative in verse form. It is called '*tal-fatt*' because its theme usually deals with a particular deed, event or legend. The theme most dealt with is the lives of well-known local personalities or a sensational or tragic event. Sometimes, it also deals with a humorous topic; but the most popular theme is the gruesome details of a murder.

Examples of themes used in this type of *għana* are: two lovers who have been caught in a storm, or the tragic murder of a child or a well-known personality. The sad stories involve a melancholic lament which is created skilfully by both the singer and the guitarist. This is done by a repetitive musical theme all along the verse rendering.

Another type of *għana* is called '*La Bormliża*' or '*għana fil-għoli*', which means 'in the Bormla style'. Bormla, also known as Cospicua, is the name of one of the three cities which make up the Cottonera area. It faces Valletta across the Grand Harbour and links the two other Cottonera cities by means of fortified walls. This type of singing has now practically died out in Malta, but has survived among Maltese emigrants in Australia. *La Bormliża* involves singing in high register, which is why in Maltese it is referred to as '*għanja fil-għoli*'. This type of singing involves short haiku-like poems normally sung by two persons who have a full voice capable of sustaining long phrases. The last type is the *makjetta*. This is usually very lively, or, as the Maltese call it, '*tal-widna*' ('pleasant to the ear').

Għana verse quatrains are made up of four-line stanzas, rhyming a, b, c and d. Each line consists of eight or seven syllables. This type of stanza is not found in Sicilian folk singing, but, according to Guzè Cassar Pullicino, is present in Greek and Spanish popular poetry. Moreover, the same form and rhyme schemes are used by the boatsmen of Rabat and Salè in Morocco.

Għana singing was also popular with women during their daily working hours. They used to sing famous verses while they carried on with their daily clothes or window washing. Usually, these verses dealt with a love story or an event which took place during the sad days of the Second World War. Moreover, the four-line stanzas used to be sung by the Maltese country women who used to spend hours kneeling side by side on the flat rooftops, preparing domestic roofs for the rainy winter season.

Għana has seen some changes after the 1953 folk song competition held for the local agrarian society by Guzè Cassar Pullicino. According to Ranier Fsadni, the effects of this change can be seen in the more elaborate singing. Moreover, it gave the skills of *għana* singing the prestige that they deserved so that they could be more appreciated even by the singers themselves. This change involved new rules, which were accepted by the majority of the *għannejja*.

The raising of the status of *għana* drew the attention of some intellectuals, especially those interested in local folklore. Thus *għana* started to be sung at festivals as well as tourist centres, such as hotels. Today an *għana* festival is being held annually at the Argotti Gardens in Floriana. This festival is attended by many Maltese interested in this type of singing, as well as tourists who happen to be on holiday in Malta. Sometimes, *għana* is included in cultural events held abroad to introduce Maltese culture during cross-cultural exchanges. Moreover, local *għannejja* tour towns and cities in Australia and Canada at the invitation of Maltese organisations where there are large Maltese communities.

Nowadays, *għana* can still be heard during the Mnarja folk festival, which is held annually in the Buskett Gardens on the night of 28 June, the eve of the feast of St Peter and St Paul. It can also be heard in a particular wine shop at Żejtun. The tradition of *għana* singing was packed away in the Maltese emigrants' luggage and taken to the new countries of adoption: Australia, the United States of America, and Canada.

Some *għannejja* have become legendary heroes: Mikiel Abela, who was popularly known as *'il-Bambinu'* ('Baby Jesus'), Frans Baldacchino and Karmenu Bonniċi, are all cases in point. Frans Baldacchino played an important role in the revival of *għana*. He was also involved in producing an *għana*-based mass targeted to coincide with the Pontiff's visit in 1990. He also took part in an *għana* prize day evening event, which

Merrymaking at the Mnarja festival during the time of the knights.

was held at a primary school at Żabbar. He sung accompanied by a children's choir.

Għana involves the playing of guitars; but in former days, a variety of musical instruments was used. These were: the *żaqq* (Maltese bagpipe), the *żavżava* or *ir-rabbaba* (friction drum), *it-tambur* (kettledrum or tambourine), *l-argunett* (mouth organ or mouth harp), and the accordion. This last instrument kept on being used until recent times. No wonder *għana* was very popular with the Maltese: it offered entertainment through music, humour and an appreciation of native skill.

Weddings (*Tiġijiet*)

In former days, it was general practice for aristocratic families to arrange marriages. This system allowed property to be inherited by a limited number of persons. Countryside girls were also expected to marry the man of her family's choice. This system broadened the family's sphere of influence.

In the countryside, when parents realised that one of their daughters was ready for marriage, they would place a pot of basil or carnation on the window ledge. On the other hand, when a young man decided to get married, during festive occasions he would wear a big, beautiful, red carnation behind his ear.

When a young man noticed a pot on the window ledge, he would try to get a glimpse of the girl while she watered the plant. He would also try to get some information on the girl's background. If he fancied her, he would go to the matchmaker (*ħuttab/a*) asking for his or her service to make contact with the girl's family. He would indicate the house or farmhouse of the girl, as well as pass on information about his property, capabilities and other information about his extended family.

The matchmaker would then visit the girl's house and try his best to bring the two families to consent to the match.

When the matchmaker informed the man that the girl's family was happy with the proposed marriage, the latter would send his sweetheart a large fish, the symbol of luck and fortune, tied with ribbons. In the mouth of the fish a ring was placed as a small gift. In some villages, it was customary for men to place any piece of jewellery instead of a ring. A meeting would then be arranged for the young couple. This would take place in the presence of the parents of both.

At this point a 'party' was organised during which neighbours and family friends were entertained with some light refreshments. On this day, the mothers of the young couple would meet to prepare a mixture of aniseed, salt, honey and herbs which they smeared on the lips of the girl. They used to believe that the girl would become affable and prudent towards her future husband. During this party, the future husband would give his girl an engraved gold ring showing clasped hands. This ring may have been inspired by a similar ring worn by Maltese upper class women to indicate that their families were supporters of the Order.

Apart from the ring, the man would also give the bride-to-be some bracelets and gold chains. The value of these objects would depend on his financial means. The girl would reciprocate by giving him a handkerchief with lace and ribbon bows. This handkerchief represented her capabilities at craft work. Marriage preparations would then start. The girl's parents would start planning her dowry while the man would start to look for accommodation for his future family. Next, a date for the wedding would be set and planning for the religious ceremony, the wedding lunch and entertainment would start.

On her wedding day, a bride used to wear a richly made dress, which included embroidery, lace and silver buttons.

A traditional Maltese wedding procession *c.*1920.

Golden ornaments were worn as well as a veil, which also included lace. The man wore a black outfit with a waist-length jacket and knee-length trousers, a white shirt and a hat in the form of a triangle.

Up till the 19th century, country brides wore dresses that were black, blue, purple and some other dark colour. By time, they started to wear a hat instead of a veil. However, some brides opted for a *faldetta* or an *għonella*. The *faldetta* was not always black; in fact, some were made from purple damask. After the wedding, they were donated to the parish church to be turned into an altar front. White dresses came into fashion at the turn of the century. At first, they became popular with Cottonera and Valletta brides, but by time, this custom spread to the other localities.

On the wedding day, the bridegroom first visited his bride's home. They then left together for the church under a canopy (*baldakkin*). This was held by either four relatives or close friends. A bridal procession then followed, which included hired musicians and singers who sang rhymes and statements honouring the couple. Behind them was a man who carried wine, a cake and candles. These items were later donated to the priest as a thank you for the service. Some members of the family used to give out confections to the passers-by. Another person carried a bowl with burning herbs. This represented the spiritual intentions of the occasion. Relatives and guests, all in their best clothes, walked at the end of the procession.

On the way to the church, the bells pealed. When they arrived, the priest would be waiting for them to start the wedding ceremony. After the ceremony, the bridal procession would make its way underneath the canopy towards the girl's house or the locality where the wedding lunch was to be held. Flowers, nuts, wheat and coins would be thrown upon them. On their arrival, it was customary for the bridegroom to do his best to enter the house first. His relatives would have been keeping the bride at the end of the bridal procession. It was a common belief that if the bridegroom did not enter before his bride, he would be henpicked for the rest of his life.

The wedding lunch followed. Usually, this was held in the house courtyard. The bridegroom ate in the company of relatives and friends, while the bride ate in a separate room. At the end of the lunch, the bride would join her new husband, drink from his wine glass and sit next to him. At this point the guests would leave left their seats, one by one, to give their best wishes to the new couple and even to present them with gifts. Presents usually consisted of gold trinkets or coins.

It is worthwhile to mention that in former days, guests sometimes cooked their lunch a day before the wedding. They would then pass the food to the house of the bride to be eaten the next day. As some couples could not afford to pay all the expenses involved in the wedding traditions, some were helped by the various confraternities. This was included in their statutes and was considered to be a popular form of charity. It was also encouraged by the church authorities.

After lunch, the bridegroom returned home with his parents and relatives. The bride remained at her parent's house for a week for the mother to have time to instruct her daughter on the role of a wife and a mother. When this week came to an end, the man's family would organise a party which was called the '*ħarġa*'. This marked the bride's new life. All the items of the dowry arrived at the new house on this same day.

A view of St Joseph church in Msida *en fête* from behind the ground fireworks mechanism.

Food

The Dark Crusty Loaf (*Il-Ħobża*)

Malta has a type of bread that is peculiarly local. At first sight, it is similar to bread found in other parts of the Mediterranean, such as in Italy, Sicily and Portugal. The Maltese bread (*il-ħobża*) consists of an outer crunchy crust with an inner part which is very soft. Some prefer to eat it when it is warm. Most Maltese like to have lunch or dinner served with a least one slice of this bread. All agree that to get the best out of Maltese bread, one has to eat it fresh, that is, it should be eaten on the same day that it is baked. There are many types of Maltese bread such as '*tas-Salib*' ('of the cross'), '*tas-Sikkina*' ('of the knife'), the '*ftira*' and '*tal-Kexxun*' ('of the drawer').

The Maltese bread recipe has not changed over the years. It is made with simple ingredients: flour, yeast, water and sea salt. In order to produce bread, the baker (*il-furnar*) and his team (usually his family members) need to have lots of patience. A love towards their trade is also a must. Production starts in the small hours of the day. The baker starts by taking a piece of *ħmira* (yeast) of the day before, which is then mixed with the day's new dough. Then the whole dough mixture is kneaded until the dough turns white. Some flour is scattered on top of this mixture, which is then covered with cloth. The

An assortment of Maltese delicacies accompanied with bread and oil.

mixture is then placed in a warm place for some hours until its volume doubles.

The next step in bread production involves a great level of skill. The baker cuts the mixture into small portions. He gives the portions the shape of a typical Maltese loaf and places them onto wooden trays covered with flour. While this process is being carried out, the oven is lit and when its temperature rises to 500 degrees Celsius, the loaves are placed inside. Baking time is expected to take about an hour and a quarter. When baking is over, the baker takes a long wooden shovel to take the bread out of the scorching oven.

Every town and village used to have its bakery (*il-forn*). In large towns, one could find more than one bakery. The town of Qormi has a reputation for producing the largest supply of Maltese bread. Although this locality hosts a large population,

The locals will vehemently claim that Maltese bread is the best in the world.

most of its bread is carried in vans to be sold in other villages and towns whose production does not meet the local demand. Qormi's bread-making tradition dates from time immemorial. It is said that when the Knights were building Valletta, the bakeries of Qormi used to supply them with bread for their members, as well as for the masons and other construction workers.

Qormi has its fair share of legends related to bakeries. One of these legends states that Qormi was a place where malaria flourished. In order to solve this problem, the people of Qormi built a number of bakeries that warmed up the air and dried out the damp. Qormi then became one of the best localities to live in, as it was the built-up area nearest to the new capital city. Its popularity in bread production led to Qormi being known as '*Casal Fornaro*' ('the baker's locality').

All bakeries are built on a similar pattern. The bakery's door, which is wide, opens straight onto a large room. Facing the door is the oven. The Maltese oven has its own characteristics. It is made of special heat-resisting stone, approximately 8 feet by 10 feet. The oven door is made of cast iron. Next to the oven is a large mixer for kneading the dough. Nowadays these have been replaced by electric machines. In front of the door, one finds a long table for displaying samples of bread and a selection of local traditional sweets made by the baker or his wife.

A baker with a good reputation for excellent Maltese bread makes two batches a day. The first one takes place early in the morning. These loaves must be ready before the housewives or workers turn up at the bakery to buy fresh bread to prepare their daily packed lunches. In former days, the first clients used to turn up after the first morning mass, which started at about half past five. The second batch consists mainly of larger loaves. Many turn up around seven o'clock to buy bread for children's school lunches or to take a loaf for the family's

Maxokk bakery in Nadur, Gozo, produces the Maltese village version of a pizza.

daily needs. If you happen to be passing by a bakery when the bread has just been taken out of the oven, you can experience a delicious smell which surely tempts your appetite.

Some bakers have their own characteristics. Some prepare Maltese bread with sesame seeds, others bake unleavened bread called '*il-ftira*'. This bread indicates the influence of Arabic and Jewish bread. It is popular with workers who like to fill it with tuna, tomatoes and vegetables. This bread is especially popular with Żabbar bakeries.

In former days, Maltese housewives used to store Maltese bread in either a wooden chest or in earthenware jars covered with wooden lids. Bread eating was, and still is, popular with the Maltese. In the past, the Maltese used to have a popular lunch called the '*kumpanaċċ*'. This consisted of small portions of food – cheese, tomato or meat – that were consumed accompanied by bread.

In some localities the word *'kumpanaċċ'* was replaced by the word *'bukkun'*. On the feast day of Our Lady of Sorrows, women were expected to beg seven small pieces of bread (called *'is-Seba' Bukkuni'*) from their neighbours or family members. Throughout the day, they used to eat only these morsels accompanied by some glasses of water. This tradition was popular among young unmarried girls.

Since the Maltese islands were never able to produce sufficient wheat to meet the demands of their population, wheat has always been imported. The Knights built silos to store grain. These are underground granaries which are found mainly at Floriana and Valletta.

In former days, in the villages one could meet men balancing a large wooden tray on their heads filled with freshly baked loaves of different sizes. This supply of bread was targeted to serve the family for several days. This tradition died out because nowadays, families living in outskirts communities are reached daily by a baker's van.

For a good part of the 20th century, when the two daily batches were ready, the baker used to take his horse and bread cart and make a round in different localities. These carts consisted of a large box with shelves, and were usually yellow in colour. Different types of bread were placed on particular shelves. On the inside of the cart's door there was also a balance to weigh the bread and next to it there were the different Maltese weights made of brass. A big knife was stored in a special wooden pocket, which was also fixed to the door.

The Maltese used to believe that bread was a blessing from God. Before the Second World War, several precautions were taken to make the most of the 'benefits' of this blessing. A case in point was when a person would sign a loaf with a cross before cutting it. The Maltese used to believe that when they needed a small piece of bread, they should not use a knife, but rather, tear off a piece with their hands. Children were instructed that when they found a piece of bread lying by the wayside, they should pick it up, kiss it and place it where it was safe from being trodden upon. All these beliefs might have originated from the association of bread with the Holy Eucharist.

The Maltese also associated bread with different religious festivities. On St Martin's day, they prepare a cloth bag and fill it with different dried and fresh nuts, and most important of all, a sweet St Martin's bread bun. This is given to children to symbolise the saint's acts of charity. Another saint associated with bread is St Anthony. There is a strong devotion among the people towards this saint, and his devotees keep a blessed small loaf which they refer to as *'il-ħobża ta' Sant'Antnin'* ('St Anthony's bread'). Holy Week, which is one of the main folkloristic events, also has a special type bread. This is in the form of a ring with sesame seeds on top and is referred to as *'il-qagħqa tal-Appostli'* ('the Apostles' bread ring'). This bread is so popular during this time of the year that it is sold from several groceries and supermarkets as well as from street vans parked next to churches on the evening of Maundy Thursday. This bread represents the bread used during the Last Supper of Our Lord and His Apostles.

Even the Knights gave great importance to bread. Every Sunday, following High Mass, the Grand Master, together with the seven Piliers, met in the Grand Master's Hall to give a weekly loaf to Rhodes families whose ancestors had left Rhodes when the Knights surrendered the island to the armed forces of the Sultan of Turkey. This loaf was known as *'il-ħobż ta' Rodi'* ('Rhodes's Bread').

Another devotion, which was introduced to Malta by the Knights, is that of St Blaise. On the feast day of St Blaise (3 February), one of the St John's Conventual Church's sextons, distributed a small bread bun the size of a hazelnut to all devotees. A bigger bread bun was distributed to those devotees who visited this church in order to kiss the saint's relic. These

The simplest of meals. Maltese bread drizzled with olive oil, tomatoes, capers and tuna is the local staple beach snack.

devotees could eat more than one loaf and drink a glass or two of wine, which was blessed as part of the saint's feast. The sexton gave St Blaise's loaves to the Grand Master, as well as to the Knights' Grand Cross. On the other hand, a loaf was sent to the residences of the Knights who missed the religious celebrations. On the same day, loaves of St Blaise bread were also blessed at another two locations at Mdina. One was the Cathedral Church of St Paul and the other was the monastery of the Benedictine nuns.

Maltese bread leftovers are also used. The farmers use these to feed poultry. Moreover, these leftovers can be turned into the very popular bread pudding (*il-pudina tal-ħobż*).

The best way to taste Maltese bread or *ftira* is to make the traditional *ħobż biż-żejt* (olive oil on bread). Together with rabbit stew, this is considered by many Maltese to be the main food of the Maltese. There are many ways of preparing a *ħobża biż-żejt*. One of the most popular ways is to rub a freshly cut tomato or tomato paste (*kunserva*) on a slice of bread, followed by a drizzle of olive oil, and a topping of tuna, olives and capers. This snack is also available in many take away vans or bar outlets.

Another, less popular, snack involving Maltese bread is to take a slice and spread it with *bigilla* – a traditional Maltese dip made from beans. Finally, a slice of bread is extremely delicious accompanied by *ġbejniet* (locally made cottage cheese or cheeselets). There are several types of *ġbejniet*: fresh *ġbejniet* (known as '*tal-ilma*'), dried *ġbejniet* (*moxxi*) and dried *ġbejniet* spiced with pepper or herbs (tal-bżar).

Ġbejniet were so common in local folk cuisine that one of the local sieges is popularly known as '*L-assedju tal-ħobż u l-ġbejniet*' ('the bread and cottage cheese siege'). Before the coming of the Knights, Malta was invaded by corsairs. They managed to take over all of the countryside, dragging many into slavery. Only Mdina resisted, due to its fortified walls. The corsairs managed to camp outside Mdina. They were planning to take Malta but

Fresh *ġbejniet*, dried *ġbejniet*, and dried *ġbejniet* with pepper.

did not want to starve the people, so they sent them Maltese bread. These loaves were rejected by the Maltese leaders and were sent back accompanied by *ġbejniet*. It is believed that during the night, St Paul was seen flying on a white horse chasing the corsairs. At dawn the corsairs' camps disappeared from sight. Mdina was saved, and so were the Maltese islands.

Honey (*L-Għasel*)

Malta has been involved with the production of honey since time immemorial. Honey is referred to as the health-giving 'gold'. The word 'Malta' derives from the Greek word for honey or 'land of honey', '*Melitos*'. This means that the production of this commodity existed during the time of the ancient Greeks. The Romans considered the production of honey as one of Malta's chief products. The Roman name for honey is also quite similar to the name the Romans used to refer to Malta, '*Melitai*'. In fact, Malta was called '*Melita*' by the Romans.

One of the major historical events that took place during Roman times involves honey. Caius Verres, a prætor of Sicily, who also governed Malta, treated his subjects very cruelly and extorted from them heavy sums of money. Cicero, the great Roman orator refers to a number of precious goods which Caius Verres carried away from the Islands. These included four hundred jars of honey, as well as large quantities of Maltese cloth, fifty cushions for sofas and a candelabra, together with the Temple of Juno's precious ornaments.

Honey remained popular with the Maltese until sugar was introduced. The climate of Malta is ideal for the production of honey because of its mild winters. Some localities, which offered bees plenty of sweet-smelling fodder, became famous for the quality of their honey. These include Fawwara in Gozo and Comino. But the most famous locality for honey

Punico-Roman apiary at Imġiebaħ, limits of Xemxija.

production is Mellieħa, as its district 'l-Imġiebaħ', meaning 'beehives', indicates.

Honey is often mentioned in old documents. A document of 1579 refers to a farmer's petition to build a wall around his hives at Mellieħa. He wished to protect his honey production from the herds of goats and flocks of sheep which were taken out to graze by the shepherds in the area. Moreover, there is an old stone apiary in Mellieħa with 40 apertures that is no longer being used.

Unfortunately, there are not so many beekeepers left in Malta, although their numbers have recently increased. Almost each season has its own typical honey. Spring is famous for the production of clover (*silla*), and at this time of year, bees produce clover honey. In early summer, the Maltese fields are rich in thyme (*saghtar*), so summer is the time for the first jars of thyme honey to appear on the market. Finally, autumn is the time for carob (*ħarrub*) honey. Each variety has its typical fragrance and colour. But besides these, bees also produce propolis, which is the ideal natural product to protect everyone from nasty colds and flu symptoms.

Jars of honey are available in open-air markets, groceries and supermarkets. Honey is still considered to be a precious commodity and it makes an ideal gift for both the local and foreign recipients.

Nougat (*Qubbajt*)

Every feast has its own particular sweet. Christmas Day has its *qagħaq tal-għasel* (honey rings), Easter has its *figolla* (a large, double biscuit pastry with honey-marzipan filling) and the towns' and villages' feast days have *il-qubbajt* (nougat). This word is Semitic and is derived from the Arabic language. Sicily,

The old display furniture for nougat selling has been retained.

Malta's neighbouring island, has a similar sweet, and it is possible that it originated during the times of Arab rule, as both Malta and Sicily experienced long years of Arab subjugation.

A bar of Maltese nougat consists of a mixture of nuts, honey and raisins. Every nougat maker has his or her own nougat mixture, which is kept secret and is safely guarded by all the members of the nougat 'factory'. All nougat makers inherit the trade from their fathers and grandfathers. Most of them hail from the town of Żebbuġ. No wonder that during a feast day, the most popular nougat hawker's cry is *'iż-Żebbuġi hawn'* ('here comes the Żebbuġ man').

We find three different types of nougat. There is honey nougat, carob nougat, and that which is made from a mixture of both these main ingredients. Nowadays, we find small bars of nougat covered with delicious chocolate. The latter were created to increase the variety of nougat available on the local market.

In former days, at the end of the locality's feast day, before returning home for a good night's sleep, the father and the rest of the family used to visit one of the stalls selling nougat (*imwejjed tal-qubbajt*) and buy a large bar to take home. It was not unusual for the family to buy one, two, or more bars of different types to suit everyone's taste. Sometimes, the father used to buy another bar or two as a 'souvenir' of the feast for his employer or workmates. Another custom, which has now died out, was for a young man to take a bar of nougat as a gift to his girlfriend's family.

Nougat is sold in highly decorated stalls set up near the parish church where the feast is being celebrated. These nougat stalls have two tables. The lower table is large and is used for displaying samples of each kind of nougat available for sale. At the end of this table there are two special small glass 'windows' for displaying larger samples of nougat highly decorated with coloured icing. On the upper table, there is a decorated scale

It is not a Maltese *festa* without the nougat stand.

and some big knives. Sometimes, these stalls are illuminated with bright lights to attract customers.

Besides the man selling nougat, next to the stall there is usually another man inviting the passers-by to taste a piece of nougat. He has a large plate in one of his hands with small pieces of nougat to offer, especially to tourists. Often, a taste of nougat is a new experience for them and some buy a large bar or two to take home and to share it with family members and friends. These nougat stalls always include the names of the makers, some of whom have become very popular.

These nougat stalls with all their characteristics add gaiety to the atmosphere in the streets or squares where they have been set up. This gaiety is enhanced by the ringing of church bells, the firing of air fireworks and the cries of the nougat hawkers. All these sounds are part and parcel of any town or village feast, be it a feast in honour of the parish saint or that organised by one of the locality's main confraternities.

In former days, every Sunday, a type of nougat sweet wrapped in silver paper of different colours was also sold from small stalls set up near a market or in a square or street next to a village's parish or conventual church.

The Market (*Is-Suq*)

In Malta we find two types of markets: open air as well as covered markets. The open air markets are more numerous and can be found all over the Maltese islands. They are usually held once a week and they start early in the day until the early hours of the afternoon. The only days when these markets are not held are when there are occasional heavy downpours. The hawkers (*il-bejjiegħa tas-suq*) are prepared for all possible weather conditions. If it starts to rain, the tarpaulin is quickly rolled out to cover all the items on the stall. Some hawkers

The hawkers start bellowing their traditional cries, aimed at attracting the attention of their visitors to the market.

also provide cover against rain for themselves and for their customers.

The hawkers start their work in the small hours of the day. Before the first rays of dawn, the hawkers begin to arrive at the market place. As they arrive, one can hear the muted creaking of carts and the whispers uttered among the hawkers. As time passes, the stalls are prepared with merchandise for sale, making it easier for the customer to pick his or her needed items. All sorts of goods on sale: underwear and clothes, leather goods, household appliances, toys, pot and pans, shoes and costume jewellery. Nowadays, one can also find a selection of highly polished beads made out of wood, plastic or coral.

After the end of the first Mass, the customers start to arrive. The hawkers start bellowing their traditional cries, aimed at attracting the attention of their visitors to the market. Mixed with these cries is the sound of CD music blaring out as the

The fish market in Marsaxlokk is Sunday's biggest open air market.

customers try one after another. Among the visitors, who find it difficult to walk between the tightly packed stalls, one is bound to see a number of housewives who have either stopped working after they tied the knot or who are now pensioners. They usually arrive at the market in the company of their children or their grandchildren.

A number of towns and villages have an open air market. A case in point is Paola, popularly known as '*Raħal Ġdid*', where a market is organised next to the town's main square. Qormi also has an open air market held on Saturdays next to the parish church of St Sebastian. Mosta, a major town to the north, has an open air market too. Birkirkara's open air market is held at one of the sides of the St Helen parish church, while Rabat's open air market is held on Sundays in a wide street facing the St Paul's parish church. Birgu's vast open air market starts outside Bormla's walls and ends next to the Żabbar Gate, and the open air market of Żejtun is held in one of the town's car parks. Victoria in Gozo has an open air market which is held in its main square, '*It-Tokk*', today called Independence Square. There are many more small open air markets scattered in various localities.

Sundays are special market days. Marsaxlokk, Malta's major fishing village, hosts Sunday's biggest open air market. Apart from the usual market merchandise, one can find a vast variety of fish for sale. This market is held along the pier. At Fortini, a district of Birgu, an open air car boot sale is held regularly. It starts in the small hours of the day and it is famous for used items. Collectors of antiques flock to this market. On Sunday afternoon, an open air market, where all sorts of items are sold, is held at Ta' Qali.

The biggest daily open air market is held at Valletta. This is Malta's best-known market and is referred to as '*il-Monti*'. This market started in one of Valletta's streets, Merchants Street. In this street there is a building which housed the *Monte di Pietà*.

Victoria's open air market, Gozo.

This official pawn-broking house dates back to the days of the Knights; the profits of this institution were devoted to the ransom of Maltese or other Christian slaves.

By time, the *Monti* market moved place. After the Second World War, it started to be held in front of St John's Co-Cathedral. As the square is rather small, the stalls used to occupy all of the square, as well as part of the narrow St Zachary street. Some complained that the crowds attending the open air market were causing 'damage' to the historical and artistic gem that is St John's. So, the market had to be moved once more. Since August 1989, *il-Monti* has gone back to Merchants Street. As this market is held every working day, it is Valletta's major shopping attraction. Locals do not only turn up to buy any necessities, but come here to socialise, to meet their friends and family members and to gossip. Some end the shopping spree with a cup of tea or coffee coupled with one or two *pastizzi* in one of the nearby cafés.

Sundays and public holidays are special days for *il-Monti*. On this day, every Maltese citizen can set up a stall and sell any merchandise without having to apply or pay for a special permit. This right has been handed over since the times of the Knights. Nowadays, one can come across a few genuine bargains, especially if the buyer is interested in caged birds, antiquarian books, tools and hardware, old furniture, and pets (especially goldfish and hamsters).

Another type of market is the covered market. The former Birkirkara covered market has now been turned into a fast food attraction. Only Valletta still has its covered market. This is simply known as *'is-Suq tal-Belt'* ('the market of the city'). It is located in Merchants Street opposite the back side of the Presidential Palace. Its roof is a work of art made of cast iron. It is a reminder of the former days of British Rule.

When Malta became a British colony, all barracks and public buildings used by the British administration were erected outside Valletta's walls. Only the Angelican Cathedral of St Paul, the Scottish church, the Royal Opera House and the Valletta market were built within the capital city's fortifications. The Valletta market's roots go back to the times of the Knights. It was held on the waterfront of the Grand Harbour – outside Porta del Monte (today's Victoria Gate) around Neptune's fountain. The British administration wished to move its locality and strong protests by the stallholders and some Valletta residents were held. Still, it had to be organised in another, more central part of the capital – in Merchants Street. Sir Gaspar Le Marchand, a governor of Malta, wanted a modern and well-equipped building to serve as a market. He wished to have a market similar to that of London's Covent Garden or Paris's *Les Halle*. A committee was set up to draw a plan. Mr Giovanni Vella had to look at the financial aspect of this project. Mr Zimelli, the then Superintendent of Public

The Victorian interior of the Valletta covered market in Merchants Street.

Works in Malta, was sent to England and France to acquaint himself with new construction technology.

When he returned, Mr Zimelli was assisted by an Englishman, Sir Charles Fox, and a Frenchman, Monsieur Victor Battard, to draw up a market plan. The construction was carried out by Salvatore Fenech. Stockport engineering firm, Emmerson and Murgatroyd of the Heaton Foundry, produced the cast iron works. This market occupied a whole Valletta block. Mr Emmanuel Galizia eventually replaced Mr Zimelli and proceeded to England to acquire more professional information regarding the new market's roof. On 30 November 1861, the Valletta market was opened to the public. It hosted 205 stalls rented at either £15 or £18 a year. There were also 72 storerooms with an annual rent of either £10 or £12.

The Valletta market was bombed during the Second World War and had to be rebuilt. Its façade, however, which originally had a flight of steps along the market's whole front, was pushed inward to create a small square. This change resulted in the loss of 45 stalls' posts. Otherwise, the building has retained all the original ironwork, as well as the wooden roofing. The fishmongers had to be given different allocations, since before the war, they used to be all lined up at the market's entrance. In the sixties, there was some restoration on its cast iron roof and entrance. In the seventies, the old chipped paving stones were replaced.

In 1981, the Valletta market, which at that time had 146 stalls selling meat, groceries, bread and fish, and employing 110 workers, was closed down. Stallholders were offered a supermarket at Beltissebħ, a district of Floriana, Valletta's suburb. This new market place offered only 50 stalls. The former Valletta market was turned into a shopping centre for Maltese products, named *'Ixtri Malti'* ('Buy Maltese'). The building has retained its exterior features but the interior has been completely restructured. In 1989, the new building's interior started to be used again as a market, but the stalls were not set up again.

The Valletta market was the best place to buy your daily necessities – butter, bread, ham, milk, meat, fish and cheese. Inside this building, one would come across butchers, grocers, greengrocers and fishmongers. While shopping, one could smell a variety of aromas, the strongest among them that of freshly baked Maltese bread. The smell of the nearby sea was offered up by the freshly caught fish, while the bursting ripe Maltese fruit and mouth-watering vegetables offered the visitor a unique smell and a pleasant sight of colours.

In the past, the Valletta market was the capital city's meeting place. Many city dwellers and people from the countryside used to visit Valletta on a shopping spree. In order to purchase their necessities, customers used to jostle between stalls. It was a building that enabled Maltese buyers to walk from one corner to the other within a few minutes. While walking, one could cast a critical eye on products and their prices along the way.

Since it has been modernised, this place has lost some of its popularity. In 2008 the Malta Environment and Planning Authority listed the covered market as a Grade 1 building. It is earmarked to be remodelled back to its former glory, back to the good old days when a visit to Valletta had to include a visit to this market place.

Shops (*Il-Ħwienet*)

In the past, shopping was mainly done in village and towns markets. Gradually, a shop or two were opened for the locals to find the items they needed. Some shops have changed with time. Others have only changed the items for sale, while some lottery stalls, kiosks and wine bars have remained untouched for decades. Many of these shops still have their hand-painted signs and traditional wooden shop-fronts. Some of these signs have become hardly legible. In these types of shops, the shopkeepers still insist on selling things over the counter rather than switching to self-service.

Some localities still have these old types of shops. One of them is Valletta. In the main street, Republic Street, we come across Caffe Cordina. This shop is situated in one of the historical buildings of Valletta facing the monument of Queen Victoria, a reminder of Malta's link with the British Empire. This shop is probably Malta's oldest established coffee shop. Its vaulted ceiling is embellished with paintings by one of Malta's leading painters, Giuseppe Calì. In the same street, further up towards the city's entrance, there is one of the City's oldest pharmacies. This shop has been modernised, however, without any major

One of the many old gold and silver shopfronts in St Lucia Street.

structural changes to the premises. Republic Street also has a corner minimarket named 'Wembley', which has preserved the original wooden green shop-front, as well as the iron staircase.

In Merchants Street, parallel to Republic Street, there is the confectionery outlet, C. Camilleri and Sons. This shop was opened in 1843 and it still sells sweets. It has since been modernised, but the old atmosphere has been preserved. In Valletta, in quite a number of back streets, such as St Paul's Street, Old Bakery Street and St Lucia Street, one can still come across a number of old shops selling various wares, from ironmongery to bedding. When one steps inside these shops, one still gets the feeling of having stepped back a century or more: only the products on sale have changed.

One of the main characteristics of Valletta is the cluster of shops, mainly in Santa Lucia Street, selling gold and silver items. Most of these shops still retain their black or dark blue wooden shop-fronts. Some of them sell modern gold and silver

The old bar signs in Strait Street hark back to its golden navy days.

items, but others deal in items of old-fashioned gold Maltese jewellery, which are really works of art.

Strait Street is being revived. Old buildings are being taken up as restaurants and wine bars. In summer, small tables are brought out onto the street and food and drink are served. This street was the former Red Light district of Valletta. But since the British soldiers and sailors left Malta, it suffered a decline. Many of its bars and entertainment spots closed down. The women who used to work as barmaids lost their jobs. Nowadays, new restaurants are opening and social night life is gradually returning to this Valletta district.

Rabat, Mdina's neighbouring locality, has some old shops in St Paul's Street. There are *pastizzi* shops with their traditional small square tables, the small oven and the ever busy shop counter. Behind this counter, there is always a kettle with boiling water ready to serve tea or coffee. Patrons come here for their *pastizzi*. Usually, they take one or two *pastizzi* and tea or coffee. The *pastizzi* are served in small glass plates, while tea and coffee are served in small glasses. While having their snack, the customers spend some time discussing the latest

These old wooden shop-fronts are like little gems dotting the local streetscape.

news, pigeon- and horse-keeping, as well as the football match results. All the walls of the coffee shops are usually covered with posters of well-known international footballers. A niche with the image of Our Lady or Jesus is always prominently displayed.

Half way down this street is an ironmongery that still has the atmosphere of bygone days. Opposite this shop, further up, there is an old shop selling gold and silver items. This shop, too, has the traditional wooden shop-front.

Victoria, Gozo's unique city, also has its fair share of old shops. In its main square, *It-Tokk,* there are some shops that still preserve their former atmosphere. One of these shops is an old corner wine and coffee shop. There are also shops selling handcrafts, souvenirs and stationery. Another cluster of old shops in this locality is found in the area around the Basilica of St George.

This old bar in Victoria, Gozo retains the characteristic Maltese floor tiles.

Some local bars are veritable time capsules.

Two other localities that have kept their old well-known confectionery shops are Msida and Ħamrun. The Busy Bee coffee shop in Msida, has been modernised, but kept its traditional atmosphere and sweets. Its white marble makes this coffee shop unique. The same can be said about Elia in Ħamrun. This confectionery and coffee shop has been enlarged, but has kept its wall shelvings filled with chocolate boxes and its counter is always full of sweets the company continues to produce for the local market.

Another type of old shop is the bar. Their names reflect the love the bar owners had for their bars. We find names such as 'Second to None Bar', 'Friend to All Bar', and 'First and Last Bar'. A bar in Victoria reflects the political sentiments the owner had towards the British: 'The Glory of England'. These bars are usually found in squares or the locality's main streets.

Some bars are well-known for the way they prepare the *ftira*. Its fillings vary from bar to bar, but the most popular are tuna, beans, capers and herbs. The bar owner tries to keep his special ingredients a secret.

The parish band clubs also have their own bars. In these bars, the patrons either play cards or watch television. They also discuss the latest street decorations for the village feast or the latest development of their club's fireworks factory. There is always the warm company of old friends who sit together after a long day at work. These men gradually return home for a welcoming hot supper in the company of their families.

Wine (*L-Inbid*)

Some believe that it was the Phoenicians who introduced vines in Malta. They planted two varieties of vines: the *Girgentina* (a white grape vine) and the *Ġellewża* (a red grape vine). By time, these two vine varieties flourished and adapted themselves to the long, hot and dry summer days and to the poor quality of soil. These two varieties are still popular with wine consumers. In the 1970s, wine production became more professional, and other varieties were introduced with the aim of satisfying the local market. But problems soon cropped up. The Maltese farmer was reluctant to switch to these new varieties as he was not ready to leave his fields unproductive for several years. On the other hand, in 1994, one of the wineries introduced a project to encourage the vine farmers to grow quality grapes. Modern planting methods and drip irrigation were looked into.

To meet the growing demands of the local market, more, new varieties of vine were planted and other grapes varieties started to be imported. After Malta joined the European Union in 2004, protective levies were lifted. As a measure for survival, the local wine producers started to look for higher quality wine production.

In Malta, the vine is not expected to produce high quality grapes before at least three years after it is planted. In winter, the plant is pruned leaving just two or three branches with their dormant buds. This agricultural activity is carried out to protect the vine from the onslaught of the winter's winds and to ensure that the following year's crop will be of better quality. In April, the stalks start sprouting new shoots. By June, grapes start developing, sheltered between the vine's leaves. During the early summer months, the grapes grow, ripening until harvest time, which is usually towards the end of August. Harvest usually starts after the feast of the Assumption on 15 August, popular known as '*Santa Marija*'. The first grapes to be harvested are the *Ġellewża,* then the *Girgentina* grapes follow. All harvesting activity must be over around the middle of September.

Harvesting grapes is a very delicate process. Grape-pickers hold the bunch of grapes in their hands, then place it gently in

A vineyard in Rabat, just below the ancient city of Mdina.

the crate. If the bunch is thrown into the crate without caution there is a risk of breaking the skin and exposing the grape. For this reason, grape-pickers are carefully selected well before harvest time. They are usually members of the extended family or close friends of the vine-grower. They start their laborious work at dawn each morning. The owner of the vineyard has to take all the necessary measures as grape harvesting must be ready before the first rains, which usually start in late September or early October.

Each harvest day, the grapes leave the vineyards on trucks that deliver them to the winery. Sometimes, trucks do two deliveries a day, depending on the amount of grapes harvested. At the winery, the grapes are weighed and the vineyard owners are paid accordingly. Then, the wine-making process starts. The white grapes go through the pressing machine. Their juice is placed in vats for fermentation, while the red grapes are placed in their fermentation vats where they are kept for about

An aerial view of a Maltese wine estate and vineyards in Ta' Qali.

Malta boasts some truly excellent award-winning wines.

a week. They are then strained. The red grapes need a different method, as the red colour of the wine is extracted from the grapes' skins. Bottling will then follow.

In Malta we find two types of vineyards. The large vineyards are found at Wardija, ir-Ramla, Marnisi, Għajn Riħana, Mġarr, Fiddien and Għollieq, while small, family-run vineyards can be found all over Malta. There are four major wine producers in Malta: Emmanuel Delicata (1907) and Marsovin (1919) are the two oldest wineries in Malta. Marsovin was later joined by Camilleri Wines. The other two are Montekristo and Meridiana. Gozo can boast of two other wineries. These are Ta' Mena and Tal-Massar. Many Maltese wine drinkers cut their own grapes from their small vineyards or vine trees in order to produce wine for their families and friends. In order to increase the level of wine production, in 2007 a new Quality Wines Produced in Specified Regions (QWPSR) system was introduced in Malta.

The vine tree is very popular in Maltese gardens. Usually, vines are planted near the main garden path, in the middle of the garden. A wooden frame (*kannizzata*) is built over the whole path for the vine branches to rest upon. During early summer, the small grapes will start to hang from these wooden frames sheltered by the large leaves of the vines. Walking along these paths under the hanging ripening grapes is a pleasant thing to do during a holiday, especially if the garden is enriched by a playing fountain or a niche at the far end. In former days, paper bags were placed around the ripening grapes to save them from hungry birds and insects.

The garden owner takes a great pride in the grapes and sees that when they are ripe enough, they are either turned into wine or placed in the centre of the dinning table, ready to be eaten after a long and delicious lunch. The best local wines are drunk in winter. In former days, when men returned home from work, they used to wash themselves and hurry off to the band club or the village's wine shop for a pint (*pinta*) of wine. Here, while they drunk wine, they met friends, exchanged the latest news about the parish or about some current topic. Political news was also included in the conversation.

It is a custom in Malta to start drinking September wine during the feast of St Martin in mid-November. In former days, wine consumers used to try to visit the village's wine shop to taste the new annual wine. They usually ordered

A Roman Italic amphora used to transport wine (Gozo Museum of Archaeology).

some nuts to be washed down by the newly produced wine. At St Paul Shipwreck church at Valletta, a confraternity of wine growers and restaurant and hotel owners was established. The members of this lay confraternity, known as '*fratelli*' used to organise a feast, every mid-November, in honour of their patron saint, St Martin. The Maltese used to joke about this confraternity's *fratelli* calling them unreliable as they are always drunk. St Paul's still houses the chapel dedicated to St Martin, even though St Martin's fraternity has now ceased to function. In this chapel, there is a large altarpiece showing St Martin together with a representation of the Annunciation.

In Malta there is no wine route, but several wine festivities are held annually. The two major wine companies organise their own wine festivals, while the villages of Qormi, Siġġiewi and Nadur organise a wine festival.

Maltese Food (*L-Ikel Malti*)

Maltese food has been influenced by French and Italian cuisines, as well as those of North Africa. The traditional dish is stewed rabbit (*fenkata*). As this takes a long time to be prepared, the rabbit meat almost falls off the bones. The Maltese love to serve the stew's rich tomato sauce with spaghetti as a first course. Nowadays, rabbit sew is also being served as a main dish with vegetables and chips or oven-cooked potatoes.

Another popular dish is roast potatoes (*patata l-forn*). This is usually served as Sunday lunch and during family gatherings. The main ingredients of this dish are onions, potatoes, water, fennel and pork chops (*kustilji tal-majjal*). Strangely, this dish is simply referred to as 'roast potatoes', even though meat is one of its ingredients. This dish, which is irresistible due to its delicious taste, is usually served with Maltese bread.

Another popular dish is ravioli (*ravjul*). The Maltese have made their own adaptations to this dish. The dough is traditionally homemade and it is filled with a mixture of eggs, ricotta (*rikotta*) or cheeselets (*ġbejniet*). Seasoning and freshly cut parsley sprigs (*tursin*) are also added. When they are ready, they are placed in boiling water on a steady, low temperature. Then, they are served with garlic flavoured tomato sauce and grated cheese. A normal serving consists of between ten to twelve ravioli pieces. Sometimes, when ravioli is filled with spinach (*spinaċi*) and ricotta, a creamy mushroom sauce replaces the traditional tomato sauce.

A typical seasonal dish is the dolphin fish or Dorado (*lampuka*). This fish is caught from mid-August to November or December. It is either served fried with chips and vegetables, as a pie, or baked with potatoes and seasoning.

Traditionally, the Maltese buy their vegetables at the local market. They usually buy seasonal vegetables for their soups.

Maltese *pastizzi* (cheesecakes) hot out of the oven.

Qassatat are pastry bags filled with either ricotta, spinach or peas.

During winter, soup is made from cauliflower, cabbage, pumpkin and kohlrabi. Another popular vegetable soup is the *minestra* that includes a quantity of pasta. There is also another version of the *minestra*: the *kawlata* – a soup which includes smoked pork.

When the family is either on a shopping spree or facing a time-consuming activity, snacks replace the main dishes. One of the most famous snacks is cheese cakes (*pastizzi*). These are very tasty, and once you try one, they become irresistible. They are made from puff pastry in the form of a bulging envelope. We find three types of *pastizzi*: ricotta (*tal-irkotta*), peas (*tal-piżelli*) or anchovy (*tal-inċova*). The last type are usually popular during Holy Week. There is another type of *pastizzi*, which is referred to as 'waxy' (*tax-xema'*). These are either ricotta or peas. The ricotta *pastizzi tax-xema'* are circular in shape, while the peas ones are shaped like half moon. Aside from *pastizzi*, are the bag-shaped *qassatat*. They are bigger and are sometimes

Honey rings have a crunchy crust filled with soft and moist treacle.

filled with ricotta or peas. Both *pastizzi* and *qassatat* are eaten slightly hot.

A tasty summer snack is *bigilla* and *galletti*. *Bigilla* is made out of broad beans (*ful*), garlic (*tewm*) and hot chilli pepper (*bżar aħmar jaħraq*). As this mixture is served in bowls, people serve themselves by means of *galletti*, which are dipped into the mixture. These *galletti* are made of semolina, are hard and blend well when dipped into the soft *bigilla*. Another snack is cheeselets (*ġbejniet*). There are three types of *ġbejniet* – soft (*tal-ilma*), peppered (*tal-bżar*) and dried (*moxxi*). The most popular are the soft *ġbejniet*. These are served with tomatoes, olive oil and freshly cut vegetables.

The Maltese are proud of their sweets. Most of the main traditional feasts are associated with particular kinds of sweets. On Christmas and New Year's Day, confectioneries sell honey rings (*qagħaq tal-għasel*). During this festive season, lunches usually finish with the traditional trifle. This has its roots in British tradition but has been adapted to suit the local taste. This is made of a combination of custard and jelly with remnants of cake. Carnival brings the *prinjolata*: a large cake in the shape of a little mound, cut into slices. This cake is covered with almonds and coloured candied peels. There are also the *perlini* made of almonds covered with an icing coating in pale colours. Lent introduces the *kwareżimal*. Ingredients include ground almonds, demerara sugar and cocoa.

On St Joseph's feast day (19 March) the *zeppole* (*sfineġ ta' San Ġużepp*, or *żeppoli*) make their appearance. These are pastries filled with sweet ricotta. They are then topped with powered sugar and nuts. Easter offers the *figolla*. It is made up of two large biscuits of various shapes held together with almond paste, covered with coloured icing sugar and decorated with a half dark chocolate egg. This important feast day is also celebrated with large chocolate Easter eggs, brown chocolate rabbits and white chocolate lambs.

Figolli are all the rage at Easter.

The town and village sell the traditional nougat (*qubbajt*). There are two types of nougat: the soft white variety, made of nuts, candied fruits and cherries, and the hard, dark brown type, consisting of a mixture of sugar and nuts. The latter has a high content of nuts with caramelised sugar.

There are also non-seasonal sweets, such as *kannoli,* which are made of tubes of sweet, deep-fried pastry filled with ricotta, sugar, spices, chocolate and candied peel. Another sweet available throughout the year is *imqaret*. To taste *mqaret* you have to come across a man frying these date-filled pastries. These are best eaten hot, straight from the pan.

Finally, the Maltese have three types of ice creams: countryside (*tal-kampanja*), grandmother's (*tan-nanna*), and cinnamon. The last is the most popular and is still served during special receptions such as christening and wedding parties. As this ice cream includes spice, it was considered to be a luxury. Some scholars are of the opinion that this type of ice cream was introduced by the Arabs.

Trade, tradition and charm - St Lucia Street, Valletta.

STRIES
OVERMANTELS
DELIA
LINOLEUMS
163
CARMELO DELIA
HOUSE
FURNISHER
163
C. DELIA
163
City
JEWELLERY
JOSE PA
164
JEWELLERY

In Ta' Qali, highly skilled craftsmen and artists handcraft each and every piece of exquisite glassware.

Bibliography

Abela, J., 'The Valletta Market', *The Sunday Times,* (19 Apr. 1981).

Abela, J., 'Traditional Maltese Boats', *Vigilo,* 19 (Feb. 2001), 22–5.

Anon., 'Carnival Sweet Heritage', Chris Grima, ed., *Day by Day, Malta and Gozo,* (Feb. 2013), 19.

Anon., 'Easter Time, Time for Sweets', Chris Grima, ed., *Day by Day, Malta and Gozo,* (Mar. 2013), 19.

Anon., 'Fenkata', Chris Grima, ed., *Day by Day, Malta and Gozo,* (Jun. 2014), 19.

Anon., 'Figolli', Chris Grima, ed., *Day by Day, Malta and Gozo,* (Apr. 2014), 23.

Anon., 'Lampuki Season', Chris Grima, ed., *Day by Day, Malta and Gozo,* (Sep. 2012), 21.

Anon., 'Maltese Traditional Trifle', Chris Grima, ed., *Day by Day, Malta and Gozo,* (Dec. 2013), 18–9.

Anon., 'Never Say No to Nougat', Chris Grima, ed., *Day by Day, Malta and Gozo,* (Aug. 2013), 19.

Anon., 'Niches – Immortal and Paternal Eyes', Peter Darmanin, ed., *Malta this Month,* (Apr. 1996), 42.

Anon., Pastizzi, A Typical Maltese Snack, Chris Grima, ed., *Day by Day, Malta and Gozo,* (Apr. 2013), 19.

Anon., 'Patata l-Forn – Maltese Roast Potatoes', Chris Grima, ed., *Day by Day, Malta and Gozo,* (Jan. 2014), 18–9.

Anon., 'Prinjolata', Chris Grima, ed., *Day by Day, Malta and Gozo,* (Feb. 2014), 19.

Anon., 'Quaint Shops of Character', Peter Darmanin, ed., *Malta this Month,* (Aug. 1996), 42.

Anon., 'Ravjul', Chris Grima, ed., *Day by Day, Malta and Gozo,* (Oct. 2012), 21.

Anon., 'Some Maltese Sweets to Taste', *Day by Day, Malta and Gozo,* (Jun. 2013), 19.

Anon., 'Soothing Soups', Chris Grima, ed., *Day by Day, Malta and Gozo,* (Jan. 2013), 19.

Anon., 'Summer Time – A Time for Some Light Maltese Food', Chris Grima, ed., *Day by Day, Malta and Gozo,* (Jul. 2013), 19.

Anon., 'Traditional Maltese Ice-cream', Chris Grima, ed., *Day by Day, Malta and Gozo,* (Aug. 2014), 19.

Anon., 'Zeppoli (Sfineġ ta' San Ġużepp)', *Day by Day, Malta and Gozo,* (Mar. 2014), 19.

Attard, A. F., 'In-Nar ta' l-Arju', *Festa Santa Marija,* Soċjetà Filarmonika Leone 2003, 47–51.

Attard, R., Azzopardi, R., *Antique Collecting in Malta,* (Midsea Books: 2008).

Azzopardi, C., 'Gozo Lace an Introduction to Lace Making in the Maltese Islands', (Gozo Press, 1992).

Azzopardi, J., 'Rubble Walls', *Vigilo,* 18 (Oct. 2000), 23–5.

Azzopardi, M., 'The Colourful Buses', Peter Darmanin, ed., *Malta this Month,* (Nov. 1999), 25.

Benoit, M., 'The Għonella – Excess Baggage', Peter Darmanin, ed., *Malta this Month,* (Apr. 1993), 37.

Benoit, M., 'Windmills – Many a Tale to Tell', Peter Darmanin, ed., *Malta this Month,* (Jan. 1994), 20–3.

Bezzina, J., 'Folklore Museum at Ta' Kola Windmill', Peter Darmanin, ed., *Malta this Month,* (Dec. 1996), 71–4.

Bezzina, J., *The Typical Farmhouse of Gozo,* Peter Darmanin, ed., *Malta this Month,* (Jan. 2001).

Bondin, R., 'Return of the Valletta Market: Another Promise to the People Kept', *The Democrat,* (21 Oct. 1989).

Borg, C., 'A Family Affair', *Let's Gozo – It's all about Gozo,* 1 (Sep. 2011), 32–5.

Carabott, S., 'Round and Round the ta' Bir Għeliem Windmill', *The Times,* (21 Nov. 2012).

Cassar Pullicino, J., *Studies in Maltese Folklore,* (Malta University Press, 1992).

Camilleri, J. C., 'Dgħajsa – the Maltese Gondola', Peter Darmanin, ed., *Malta this Month,* (Nov. 1994), 41.

Camilleri, J. C., 'The National Colours', Peter Darmanin, ed., *Malta this Month*, (Aug. 1993), 61.

Cassar Pullicino, J., 'Carnival, a Colourful Spectacle', Peter Darmanin, ed., *Malta this Month*, (Feb. 1994), 37.

Cassar Pullicino, J., 'Norman Legends in Malta', *Scientia*, (11 Apr. 1945), 152–65.

Cassar Pullicino, J., 'Old Customs in Retrospective', Peter Darmanin, ed., *Malta this Month*, (Jul. 1999), 54.

Cassar Pullicino, J., 'Oral Poetry in Sung Form', Peter Darmanin, ed., *Malta this Month*, (Nov. 1996), 56.

Cassar Pullicino, J., 'Superstitions Compared', Peter Darmanin, ed., *Malta this Month*, (Apr. 1999), 54.

Cassar Pullicino, J., 'The Faldetta', Peter Darmanin, ed., *Malta this Month*, (Jan. 1998), 56.

Cassar Pullicino, J., 'The Protective Eye', Peter Darmanin, ed., *Malta this Month*, (Oct. 1997), 56.

Cassar Pullicino, J., 'The Traditions of a Maltese Feast', Peter Darmanin, ed., *Malta this Month*, (Jul. 1997), 56.

Cini, G., 'Baroque Stone Carvings Underscore Valletta's Heritage', *The Times* (21 Jan. 2002).

Cremona, M., 'Quaint Shops of Character', Peter Darmanin, ed., *Malta this Month*, (Jan. 1994), 46.

Cutajar, J., 'Bright colours of a winter Carnival', Peter Darmanin, ed., *Malta this Month*, (Feb. 1997), 27–30.

Fenech, N., 'All About Maltese Houses', *The Times*, (23 Jan. 2008).

Flores, Ch., 'The Elegant Dgħajsa and the Regatta', Peter Darmanin, ed., *Malta this Month*, (Sep. 1994), 24–7.

Fsadni, Fr. M., 'The "Girna" Corbelled Stone Hut', Peter Darmanin, ed., *Malta this Month*, (Nov. 1993), 61.

Gatt, B., Reflections of a luzzu, Peter Darmanin, ed., *Malta this Month*, (Jan. 1998), 49–51.

Graham, H., J., Cecil Higgins Art Gallery and Museum, (Cecil Higgins Art Gallery and Museum: 1987).

Grima, R., The Valletta Market, *The Sunday Times*, (19 Apr. 1981).

Jaccarini, C. J., 'Ir-Razzett, the Maltese Farmhouse', *Vigilo*, 14 (Jun. 1999), 27–30.

Lanfranco, G., 'Changing Maltese Marriage Traditions', in Woman's World and Weddings Supplement, *The Sunday Times,* (7 Mar. 1993).

Leopardi, E. R., 'Malta's Heritage', (Malta, 1969).

Mizzi, P., 'Maltese Furniture – Il-Gradenza', *Heritage,* p.1580.

Mizzi, P., 'Maltese Furniture – The Coffer – Is-Senduq', *Heritage,* p.1246.

Portelli, P., 'Rubble Walls', Peter Darmanin, ed., *Malta this Month,* (Jul. 2000), 25.

Sammut, L., 'Spare the Market', *The Sunday Times,* (12 Apr. 1981).

Strickland, A., 'Balconies – Their Origin', Peter Darmanin, ed., *Malta this Month,* (May 1993), 25–8.

Strickland, A., 'Maltese Door Knockers', Peter Darmanin, ed., *Malta this Month,* (Jul. 1998), 25.

Terribile, T., 'Stone Crosses', *Vigilo,* 12 (Oct. 1998–Jan. 1999), 27–9.

The Sunday Times, (14 Aug. 2005).

The Sunday Times, (25 Jun. 2006).

The Sunday Times of Malta, (2 Nov. 2014).

The Times, (30 Apr. 1981).

The Times, (15 Oct. 1983).

The Times, (25 Jul. 2005).

The Times, (4 Aug. 2005).

The Times, (15 Aug. 2007).

Times of Malta, (28 Jul. 2014).

Zammit, V., 'Countryside Chapels', Peter Darmanin, ed., *Malta this Month,* (Jan. 1995), 25–6.

Zammit, V., 'Il-Karrozin, the Horse-Drawn Cab', Peter Darmanin, ed., *Malta this Month,* (Feb. 2003), 32.

Zammit, V., 'The Colourful Maltese Dgħajsa', Peter Darmanin, ed., *Malta this Month,* (Apr. 2005), 8–10.

Index

A

B

C

D

E

F

G

H

I

K

L

M

N

O

P

Q

R

S

T

U

V

W

X

Z

Additional Reading

www.bdlbooks.com

A Taste of Malta

Malta a Brief History

Malta Gozo & Comino
in 4 languages

Musical Instruments of the
Maltese Instruments

Ħaġar Qim & Mnajdra
Prehistoric Temples
Qrendi

Archaeological Walks
on Gozo

The Maltese Cart-Ruts
Unraveling an Enigma

Cart-Ruts
and their Impact on the
Maltese Landscape

Roman Malta
The Archaeological Heritage of
the Maltese Islands

Malta
Prehistory and Temples

Malta
Phoenician, Punic, and
Roman

Malta
The Medieval Millennium

The Ħal Saflieni Hypogeum
Paola

The Żejtun Roman Villa
Research • Conservation • Management

Ġgantija
The Oldest Free-Standing Building in the World

Malta before History
The World's Oldest Free-Standing Stone Architecture

The Knights of Malta

Malta
The Order of St John

The Grand Masters of Malta

The Fortifications of Malta by the Order of St. John
1530–1798

Hospitaller Malta
1530–1798

1565
The Great Siege of Malta

Naval Activities of the Knights of St John
1530–1798

The Manoel Theatre
A Short History

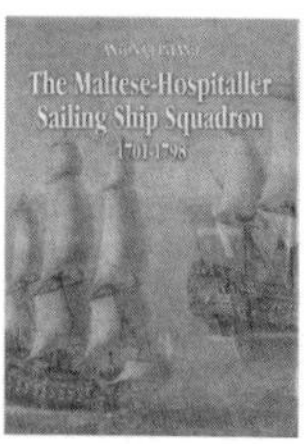

The Maltese-Hospitaller Sailing Ship Squadron
1701–1798

The Palaces of the Grand Masters in Malta
Valletta • Verdala • San Anton

The German Langue of the Order of Malta

The Last Corsairs of Malta
An Incredible True Story

The Order of Malta Exposed

The Story of Valletta
A Companion to the City

The Siege of Malta
Matteo Perez d'Aleccio's Frescoes at the Grand Master's Place, Valletta

Baroque Painting in Malta

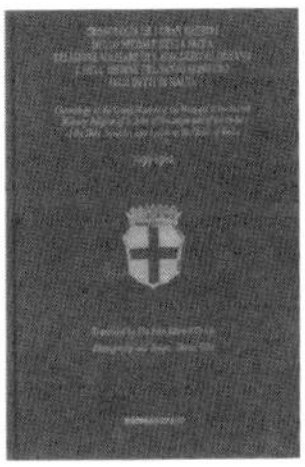
Chronology of the Grand Masters

Armoury of the Knights

The Coinage of the Crusaders and the World of Islam

Toni Bajada
The Maltese Messenger of the Grand Master

The Coinage of the Knights in Malta

Valletta
Porta Reale and Environs

Witchcraft, Sorcery and the Inquisition

The Conventual Church of the Knights of Malta

The Maritime History of Malta

Malta Surrendered
An Eyewitness Account of Napoleon's Invasion in 1798

The Saga of the French Occupation
Malta, 1798–1800

A Taste of History
The Food of the Knights of Malta

Legacy of an Order in Malta
360°

Magdalene Nuns and Penitent Prostitutes

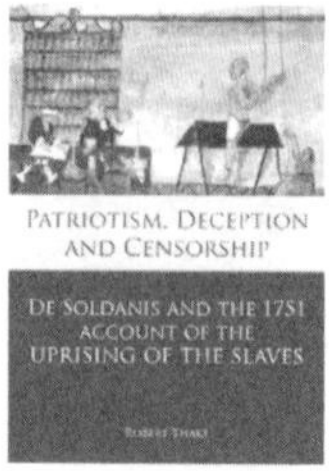

Patriotism, Deception and Censorship

Printing in Malta
1642–1839

A Concise History of Malta

A Hundred Wayside Chapels of Malta & Gozo

Gozo
The Roots of an Island

The Gran Castello at Rabat, Gozo

The Malta Coastal Walk
A Wonderful walk around the entire coast of Malta

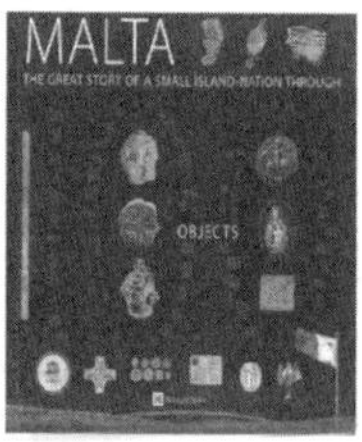

Malta
The Great Story of a Small Island-Nation through 100 Objects

Mdina
A History of its Urban Space and Architecture

The Public Gardens and Groves of the Maltese Islands

Strait Street
Malta's 'Red-Light District' Revealed

A History of the Malta Police
1800–1964

Saint Paul in Malta

Victoria
A Portrait of a City

The Brocktorff Mapmakers

Uncommon
Malta + Gozo

The Inquisitor's Palace
Vittoriosa

Vanity, Profanity & Worship
Jewellery from the Maltese Islands

The Ghosts of Malta

Gozo Lace
An Introduction to Lace Making in the Maltese Islands

Murder in Malta
A Chronicle of Homicide Cases
Volume 1: 1800–1966

Folktales of Malta and Gozo

The Making of Malta

The Story of the Malta Buses

A Catalogue of Maltese Picture Postcards

Malta During the British Era

Operation Pedestal
The Story of the Santa Marija Convoy

Malta and British Army Infantry Regiments
1800–1979

Malta Drydocks
1963–2010

Destination Malta
The Surrender of the Italian Fleet, September 1943

Screwball Beurling
Malta's Top Scoring Fighter Ace

Malta Spitfire Aces

Malta's Early Warning System during World War II

Raiders Passed
Wartime Recollections of a Maltese Youngster

Royal Navy Tugs at the Grand Harbour Malta

HMS *Hibernia, L-Arbanja* at the Grand Harbour Malta

The Guns and Gunners of Malta

The Battle of Malta
An Epic true Story of Suffering and Bravery

The Quality of Malta
.Fashion and Taste in Private Collection

Caravaggio
Art, Knighthood, and Malta

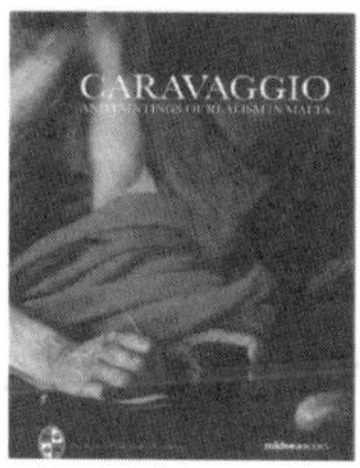

Caravaggio
and Painting of Realism in Malta

Understanding Caravaggio

Paintings at the National Museum of Fine Arts in Malta

Maltese Prehistoric Art
5000–2500 BC

Mattia Preti
Beyond the Self Portrait

Mattia Preti
The Triumphant Manner

Mattia Preti
Faith and Humanity

The Conservation of the Artistic Patrimony in Malta during World War II

Memento Mori

Cooking Maltese Cuisine

25 Years in a Maltese Kitchen

The Way we Ate
Memories of Maltese Meals

Party Politics in a Fortress Colony
The Maltese Experience